PLANTING
THE SEED OF
HOPE

A CELEBRATION OF PRAIRIE LIFE

PLANTING
THE SEED OF
HOPE

ELAINE FROESE

All scripture quotations, unless otherwise indicated, are taken from the HOLY BIBLE, NEW INTERNATIONAL VERSION®. NIV®. Copyright© 1973, l978, l984 by International Bible Society. Used by permission of Zondervan. All rights reserved.

Book design by Relish Design, Winnipeg.
Cover photo: Doug Gray.
Editor: Barbara Edie, RiverRoad Communications.
Printed and bound in Canada at Friesens.

LIBRARY AND ARCHIVES CANADA CATALOGUING IN PUBLICATION

Froese, Elaine
       Planting the seed of hope : a celebration of prairie life / Elaine Froese ; Barbara Edie, editor.

Originally published in the author's column Seeds of Encouragement, in Grainews.
Includes bibliographical references.
ISBN 10: 0-9736984-0-3
ISBN 13: 978-0-9736984-0-4

1. Rural families--Prairie Provinces. 2. Farm life--Prairie Provinces.
3. Communication in the family--Prairie Provinces. 4. Hope. I. Edie, Barbara
II. Title. III. Title: Seeds of Encouragement. IV. Title: Grainews.

S522.C3F76 2005   306.85'2'09712   C2005-901232-3

*To Lois, Ken, John, Jake, Kathy, Mark, Floyd,
and a multitude of faithful readers
who have encouraged me along the way.*

*To my loving husband, Wes, who supports
me as I travel to encourage others.*

CONTENTS

CELEBRATING

PREFACE

COMMUNICATING, CONNECTING AND CELEBRATING

In early 1995, I received a phone call from an acquaintance who was dying of cancer. That call was the beginning of my column "Seeds of Encouragement" in the farm paper *Grainews*. "I've been watching the way you write about family, and I want you to take my place," said Marie Salway, who passed away in March 1995 after 17 years as a columnist.

In 2004, I received a phone call from a farmer named Mark, who farms west of Jasper! "Elaine I want to buy your book."

"Well, then Mark, I guess I better write one!"

My passion is to encourage farm families and prairie people to be intentional about the choices they make for their lives. I've chased cows, run the combine, and watched the sky for hail clouds, just like my readers have. I love to read inspiring stories!

This book is a sampling of the themes we walk through each year as families in business, and people in transition. My journey includes depression, grief, adoption, hailstorms, bumper crops, great conversations and unexpected gifts.

Communication is one of my strengths as a professional speaker, writer and coach. I have had the honour of working with families in the sacred place of deep sharing. I want people to connect in healthy ways with each other, and my writing is geared to W.O.O. – winning others over. We also need to have fun; celebrations in our life that mark special times. Are you looking for new ways to celebrate life?

Many people have asked me where I get my ideas. I just listen and observe. If you see your story reflected in these pages, I hope that you will plant your own seeds of encouragement by sharing with others. Use the Ponder and Plant sections for reflection, and action. As Robert Hastings has written, "Enjoy the journey, the station will come soon enough."

COMMUNICATING

CHAPTER 1

RELEASING YOUR STRESS

TALK KINDLY TO YOURSELF...
OCTOBER 1995

"A joyful heart is good medicine." – Proverbs 17:22

As the garden is put to bed for the winter, and crop work nears completion our thoughts turn to other things. But, are these happy, self-affirming thoughts? The way we talk to ourselves has a big effect on how we feel and how we see things happening around us. Positive self-talk is saying "I can," setting your mind to meet the challenge at hand.

Parents of young children are often challenged with replacing put-downs with building comments like "Yes, you can do it!"

Even adults get trapped with "I blew it,"rather than "Next time I'll get it right." The way we talk to ourselves, our self-talk, is our choice. We can choose to be positive and see the glass of water as half-full, or take the negative approach and see it as half empty.

There is also the GIGO factor. Garbage In means Garbage Out. What kinds of things are you feeding your mind? Someone once said that the two biggest factors for our happiness in life are the people we meet and the books we read.

Strong families practice good communication skills which enhance positive self-talk. Are you quick to snuff out negative name-calling or labels in your conversations? Try changing the comment "If only I would have" to "Next time I will." Can your family count on you to listen intently to their feelings? Does your body language (affection, eye contact, open arms) communicate acceptance?

A wonderful birthday letter from a friend encouraged me to "lighten up." Take stock of your thought life and find moments of joy in your journey. Here are some ideas:

- **Sing or whistle a happy tune.** My father-in-law was easily found on our yard if we would just listen for his whistling.
- **Sing along with the radio or join a community choir.**
- **Connect with a friend.** Phone calls, the coffee shop, or a handwritten letter bring good news.
- **Hang around with positive people.**
- **Read something inspirational.** Feed your soul and spirited self-talk will follow.
- **Laugh.** I delight in listening to my son read his joke book. Look for humour in everyday situations and share funny situations with others.
- **Craft and create.** Whether your forté is fancy wood-working or wool making, something of beauty creates energy and enjoyment. Make a list of fun things you enjoy doing, and do them! Your kids and grandkids would love to fulfill your list with you!
- **Look up!** Whether you are waiting to see the Northern Lights, the stars or the birds, appreciate the peaceful wonder around you. Say: "Wow, that's awesome" to yourself.
- **Play!** Take a play break.

Children have so much energy because they don't get stuck at one task they change gears often. Find moments of joy, a few minutes or a few hours every day. Learn to laugh at yourself in a kind way. Talk to yourself with positive comments and say with fervor "I like myself!" You are lovable and capable. Lighten up!

THE UPSIDE OF DEPRESSION
SEPTEMBER 1999

"Failure is an event, not a person." – Zig Ziglar

"My dad is taking "happy pills" and he's a new man. I'm so glad he's finally facing his depression and getting treatment!"

"Thanks for the tape on depression that you shared. I've had a really tough year, but I'm starting to feel better."

"I've never seen this farmer so low...he's finally getting medical help for his depression."

These snippets of conversation became a strong cord of encouragement to me as people shared how they were walking among those coping with depression.

The harvest season may be difficult for many farm families, but don't lose hope. Stories of beef producers refusing to get out of bed to feed their cattle set off alarm bells that circumstances or losses have become too big with which to cope.

Recognize the symptoms of depression and get help through a complete diagnosis by your doctor.

Here's a brief list of symptoms to watch for:
- Chronic fatigue
- Disturbed sleep
- Appetite changes
- Loss of interest or pleasure in life
- Irritability, sadness or chronic anger
- Feelings of despair, worthlessness or inadequacy
- Increased thoughts of death or suicide.

You don't need the entire list of symptoms to be depressed. I had a serious depression in 1984. Later, after my mom's death, I asked a doctor to check why my energy level was so low, but the paper test she used confirmed that I was not depressed.

I encourage families to get good medical help. Don't try to keep depression a family secret. Depression is an illness which

> *"And now, God, do it again – bring rains to our drought-stricken lives so those who planted their crops in despair will shout hurrahs at the harvest, so those who went off with heavy hearts will come home laughing, with armloads of blessings."* – Psalm 126:4-6 Msg.

can be overcome when properly treated. Enlist the support of caring friends and family. When a person is depressed, the entire family is affected, so embrace everyone with gentleness, kindness and a non-judgmental attitude.

I did a radio interview for Connecting Points about walking alongside someone who is depressed. That interview is captured on CD available at my website, www.elainefroese.com.

You can call your local Canadian Mental Health Association for more information on coping with depression. I like the book *Dark Clouds, Silver Linings* by Archibald Hart. The book is now out of print, but check your local bookstore or library for resources about depression.

I agree with Hart that depression doesn't have to rule your life, but left untreated, depression can cripple you emotionally and physically. Traumatic life events, stress or tension can cause depression. Harvest time is always an adventure, but this year a real stressor for many farm families. Release those tension valves. Talk about your feelings and seek expert help.

Combines and feeder chains may break down, but people are not machines. I hate the term "nervous breakdown"; it is depression and it is treatable. May God give you the strength, courage and wisdom to find healing during the stresses your family is facing this harvest, and always.

Asking to Get Unstuck
November 1999

"Do not be anxious about anything, but in everything, by prayer and petition, with thanksgiving, present your request to God." – Philippians 4:6 (NIV)

The year 1999 will likely be remembered as the year of "getting stuck", but it has nothing to do with tractors, it's about moving your farm family towards transferring the farm. Media reports about farmers getting older, and billions of dollars worth of farm land changing hands in the next 10 years don't get to the heart of the problem.

Why are so many farm families stuck with a farm that they don't seem to be able to move on to the transfer process?

Planning for transfer isn't happening because "there is no successor" says Doug Duff, who works with Alberta Agriculture. Duff sees a widening age gap between the group leaving farming, and those coming in. He is meeting "model farmers" who are unsure if they should encourage their children to come home. Did anyone ask the children what they want?

"The problem of pre-conceived ideas happens when you fear the worst, and don't want to go down that track, yet that path might give the family a viable option," says Donna Hastings, Manitoba Agriculture's Family Living Specialist. Hastings says the mere fact that they are moving [asking] will help them generate options for the farm.

It's a three-step process of talk, write, and implement.

Here are some of the main reasons for getting "stuck" and not asking for what you want to have happen on your farm:

1. **Ignorance.** You just don't know all the options available. Call your local agriculture office and they'll get you started. "There is no lack of resources out there to help families," Duff emphasizes. Manitoba has "Managing the Present... Planning the Future" and "Family Farm Business Advisor" manuals for farm families and their professional advisors.

2. **Limiting or inaccurate beliefs.** There's a myth that says: "Be careful what you ask for, you may just get it." Unhealthy home life experiences may make you feel that asking for what you want is just too risky.

3. **FEAR.** The family farm is a family entwined with a business. There is fear of rejection, looking stupid, fear of being vulnerable or powerless, fear of humiliation or punishment. Fear of a spouse leaving and fear of owing each other forever can also keep you from moving forward.

4. **Low self-esteem.** Are you avoiding talking about farm transfer because you feel you are unworthy of love, happiness, and fulfillment? You just don't feel adequate to face your fears and create the kind of life you want. You are worth it!

5. **Pride.** "Many of us, especially men, get stuck in our pride," say Jack Canfield & Mark Victor Hansen, authors of *The Aladdin Factor.* "We are supposed to figure it out by ourselves." Wrong! A family farm that has seen many generations labour with love is not easily transferred to a stranger. That said, selling the farm does not mean you have failed your great-grandfather. He is dead ... and you are alive seeking a life with meaning and fulfillment.

How do you start asking for what you want?

- **Conquer your fears.** Realize that you create all your fears. Check out your doubts and fantasies. Imagine transferring the farm with everyone talking, listening, and treating each other respectfully.
- **Ask yourself:** What's the worst/best thing that could happen? Could I survive it?
- **Talk positively to yourself.** Ask God for help.
- **Just do it!** Read *Feel the Fear and Do It Anyway* by Susan Jeffers.
- **Build up to the big stuff slowly.** "Each day do a little more asking" recommends Canfield. His book *The Aladdin Factor* gives many practical insights to learning how to ask for

what you want and need. Transfer those ideas to your farm family.

- **Don't take "no" personally.** Learn to re-frame the meaning of rejection by making it the next step to a new possibility.
- **Be persistent.** It's a numbers game according to Canfield and Hansen. Eventually you'll get to what you are asking for if you persevere by asking people. Keep working on getting unstuck.

Farm family transfers can be a good experience if everyone is willing to ask for what they need, or a huge frustration if members are unwilling to talk. Find the chains of desire for change in your family, anchor them well with good faith, and pull in the same direction – smoothly and steadily. Ask and you will receive.

BSE ANXIETY IN THE NEUTRAL ZONE
MARCH 2004

"It not so much that we're afraid of change or so in love with the old ways, but it's that place in between that we fear…It's like being between trapezes. It's Linus when his blanket is in the dryer. There's nothing to hold on to."
– Marilyn Ferguson, futurist

I overheard a cattle farmer confiding that "It's hard to get used to living with deep fear." His anxiety was echoed by a Saskatchewan rancher who said it was tough feeding worthless cows during the January cold snap, not knowing how much longer he would have to wait for open borders.

Change consists of endings, the neutral zone, and new beginnings. In the case of the Bovine Spongiform Encephalopathy (BSE) crisis, the ending happened on May 20, 2003 when things really changed. Many farm families, cattle producers and other livestock producers have felt stuck, frustrated…and grief-stricken. So many things out one's control. The not-knowing of where the new beginning will be. What will happen?

We are in transition.

William Bridges, author of *Managing Transitions, Making the Most of Change*, calls the middle phase of the transition process "THE NEUTRAL ZONE." This is a frustrating and anxious place to be. It happens when I coach farm families who are trying to decide if they should pass the farm on to the next generation, or find a new vision and sell out. It's the place where anxiety rises and motivation fails. Things are unclear and foggy in the neutral zone; people pine for the old days and some really want to move forward and move on.

When people understand that it takes time to move from the ending stage, through the neutral zone, on to new beginnings, they can start to get a grip. "People need to recognize that it is natural to feel somewhat frightened and confused in this no-man's land," says Bridges.

Are you going to grab the bull by the horns and control what is in your control? Can you keep positive by looking at a bigger picture for your situation? What new roles or systems do you need to create in order to get through this time in the wilderness?

It is especially important to try to rebuild a sense of identification with other producers and connectedness with one another.

Use the neutral zone creatively.What short term goals can you aim for to give you some sense of achievement and movement? Are their long overdue creative projects that you can feel good about doing? I'm sure the media would love to promote a good news story about coping with the BSE crunch. What discoveries or innovations have you heard people use to make it through? This tough time is forcing people to look at new markets and new ways of doing things. There are opportunities to brainstorm to find new answers to old problems. Farmers have always fostered a deep spirit of invention and entrepreneurship. Maybe we will come out of this waiting time better able to manage the next transition! Talk about the fear. Stay connected with your family. Know the anxiety you are feeling is a normal for being in the neutral zone of change. Focus on the daily chores and goals you know you can meet.

Consumers who have shown support to producers with their beef buying dollars have been encouraging. Cattlemen are being creative and innovative in how they keep their stock in good shape while we all wait. Farm families are specialists in transition management, but this BSE challenge grows harder as the bills to be paid mount up.

Find strength by connecting to your families and community.

As the title of Dr. Nikki Gerrard's research on the resiliency of farm families says: *What Doesn't Kill You Makes You Stronger.* While we are all hoping and praying for closure of the neutral zone and the opening of the border, let's listen to the unspoken fears of those around us. Talk about your anxiety. Call your Rural and Farm Stress Line to vent your frustration. In Manitoba the number is 1-866-367-3276. Saskatchewan readers can call 1-800-667-4442, and in Alberta call 1-877-303-2642. In Ontario call 1-888-451-2903.

May our prayers be answered soon.

GET BITTER OR GET BETTER
FEBRUARY 2003

I was angry with my friend;
I told my wrath, my wrath did end.
I was angry with my foe,
I told it not my wrath did grow.
– William Blake, A Poison Tree

"Man, I can't believe my Dad, every time I make a mistake, he just can't accept my apology, and he keeps track for years!" Many farm families are saddled with an invisible load on their backs. Everyday they carry the baggage of hurt, caused by a pattern of family members who just can't seem to let go of past offenses. Forgiveness is one the critical issues that farm families need to take a hard look at, so why do they avoid it?

Accepting the fact that you are hurt is one thing, but the tough part about forgiveness is that it is the offended (you) who has to seek the forgiveness of the offender (another family member). "Forgiveness is difficult because the person who is hurt does the forgiving and not the person being forgiven," Tim Lahaye and Bob Philips write in *Anger is a Choice.*

We don't forgive and forget. We remember, but we have a choice of what we do with the memories. LaHaye says, "I can let my memories lie and move on in my life, or I can let my memories over-power me. Forgiveness is letting go. It is the relaxation of your death grip on the pain you feel. Or as Archibald Hart puts it: "Forgiveness is surrendering my right to hurt you back if you hurt me."

You choose to forgive. It is an act of your will. Lack of forgiveness is the second biggest obstacle to succession planning according to Tom Hubler of Hubler Family Business Consultants (www.hublerfamilybusiness.com). Hubler, a family business specialist uses a two-day process to help families understand the issues that need to be dealt with. His Family Forgiveness Ritual™ focuses on forgiveness, absolution and a celebration of the family and its values.

So, would you like to revive your marriage? Would you like to feel love for your family?

Forgiveness involves a commitment to three things according to Jay Adams:

1. I will not use it (the offense) against my mate or family in the future.
2 I will not talk to others about my mate or gossip about my family.
3. I will not dwell on it. To dwell on past hurts, as Lahaye says, "is like ripping your scabs to see if your cut is healing."

"Forgiveness is not holy amnesia that erases the past ... instead it is the experience of healing that draws the poison out. You may recall the hurt, but you will not relive the hurt," notes David Ausburger. To be able to forgive, we have to look the issue of hurt directly in the face. The reasons for a lack of reconciliation may be:

- death of the offender ... Dad's gone, but the hurt lingers
- denial, refusal and rejection by the offender: "I didn't do anything wrong to hurt you!"
- fear or lack of skills, energy or motivation. "I can't ask for an apology or forgiveness that's too impossible!"
- unforgiveness on your part. "I will never let go of what that person did to me."

How do you get motivated to seek forgiveness and move your farm family forward?

Decide to make the first move. Seeking healing by asking for forgiveness is an act of will – a choice.

Don't wait until you feel like it. Do you only go to feed the cows when you feel like it? Deal with the manure in your life that is keeping you down.

Insights from Lahaye to consider:

1. I have had trouble forgetting.
2. I've had a hard time forgiving these people.
3. This situation really frosts me!
4. Resentment would accomplish…
5. Revenge would accomplish…
6. Regarding the offenses above, I am not willing ... or I am now willing to choose to forgive them.
7. I will start acting lovingly toward those who hurt me by…and then would work towards…

A women at a farm crisis meeting once said: "Mom always told me that I had a choice in how to respond what happened to me in my life. I could get bitter, or get better!" Without forgiveness life is governed by an endless cycle of resentment and retaliation. Perhaps your family is ready to talk about that "undiscussabull" – the hurt that needs to be acknowledged and forgiven, and let go. Forgiveness is one of those "soft issues" farm families get frustrated with when they are "too frosted to forgive."

> *"Bear with each other and forgive whatever grievances you may have against one another. Forgive as the Lord forgave you."* – Colossians 3: 13

Call your clergy for assistance, or ask a facilitator to coach your family. Healing is the goal that will move your family forward.

LIVING WITH POSITIVE UNCERTAINTY
OCTOBER 2004

"He who dwells in the shelter of the Most High will rest in the shadow of the Almighty. I will say of the Lord, He is my refuge and my fortress, my God, in whom I trust."
– Psalm 91:1, 2 (NIV)

I always pay close attention when conversations from completely different places have a common thread. I have just walked by fields of wheat that refuse to ripen; I have listened to stories of desperate people seeking legal advice for exiting the cattle farm; I have heard stories of people needing shelter from adversity – sad stories of frustrated farmers who avoid talking about the future altogether.

We are all farming with uncertainty. "We have a choice about how we deal with uncertainty, we can be positive and create more possibilities," says Carol Gelatt, author of *Creative Decision Making Using Positive Uncertainty.* She encourages people to be focused yet flexible about what they want. Be aware and yet wary of what you know, and don't become bogged down by too much data.

Too much data! There seems to be a trend of farm families being paralyzed with too much paperwork, plans and possibilities – action plans that are sitting on the kitchen table or stuffed in the office drawer.

Do you believe that you have options? Beliefs have a huge impact on how we see things. Gelatt suggests that we be realistic about what we believe: "Dread precisely, dream and believe greatly!"

What is stopping or inhibiting you from taking action? If you are overwhelmed with too much information or data, set some boundaries for "enough is enough." Give yourself permission to stop collecting information.

Gelatt strongly believes: "Positive uncertainty increases the opportunity for expanding future possibilities. The unknowable future is not the unthinkable future. There are three types of futures ... the probable, the preferable, and the possible."

Many farm families are facing a future with fear. They are scared that someone else's decisions are going to impact them. Some families are so stuck that they make no decisions to move forward and that, in itself, is a decision by default. Ask: What else can I do? What other options can happen?

Make a "big list of little things that you could do day to day to improve the quality of your life. Make a little list of big things that could happen to achieve your goals," Gelatt suggests. The little things will help you ride the rollercoaster of life. Ride the highs and the lows and remind yourself of the things you can do to feed your energy.

To find shelter, Sandra Krebs Hirsh's book *Soultypes* suggests:

- Pull inward and consider all the hopeful possibilities.
- Be direct with others and letting them know where you stand.
- Assess what's important to you, confirm your cherished values.
- Cut out distractions to allow space for reflection and solitude.
- Allow yourself to rest to nurture your soul.
- Find ways to acknowledge and deal with your emotions.
- Reassess reality, review what can and cannot change.

Sharing is a way of finding shelter and support. Speaking about your fear and storytelling about what life looks like for you will help you see many possible outcomes. "Hey, I never thought of that" is a wonderful gift to farm folks who are stuck. Counting your blessings with an attitude of gratitude helps you appreciate the little things that lift you up. Look up, especially when you feel stuck. May the hand of God pull you from despair.

> *"To understand is to forgive – even oneself."*
> – Alexander Chase

CHAPTER 2

WORK STYLES

WHO PUT MY LIFE ON FAST FORWARD?
AUGUST 2002

"It is often just as sacred to laugh as it is to pray."
– Chuck Swindoll

My favourite farmer and I have had a lot of laughs reading Phil Callaway's latest book *Who Put My Life on Fast Forward?* Farm families across the bald prairie could use some laughter and lightness in their lives this fall. It's been a tough year for many. September brings a new whirl of community expectations after harvest winds down. The choices of chores, sports, music, 4-H, care for family, and community committees are pressing all of us. We are working really hard at making a living, nurturing our family, and investing in healthy communities. Our life tape is spinning too fast.

The need is not the call. Each one of us has to be really conscious and clear about the choices we make with our time. Don't "should on yourself" with " I should help out, I should be able to do it all, I should be able cope with 80-hour weeks!"

Ideas for pushing the pause button:

- **Listen to how your body feels.** Does the decision to get involved feel heavy...or light? Try to connect your head with the passions of your heart.

- **Write down the 10 most important things to you in your life this season.** This helps you focus on your priorities for you at this chapter in your life. You might feel unravelled when you realize you aren't doing anything remotely connected to what is on your list! Keep reviewing it.

- **Listen to your family.** Have a family chat around a really big bowl of popcorn and listen intently to each other. The person with the salt shaker gets to talk. Ensure everyone is clear about other's expectations for the family calendar. Talk about people expectations, and performance. Set limits and boundaries for the number of activities in the week.

- **Invest in memories.** Create your own family tales. Plan a date night with your mate; let the kids have you all to themselves for a couple of hours. Time needs to be invested. Fun can be had for little money.

- **Keep track.** It was a shocker for me to realize months had passed since our last date night. "Usefulness is nine-tenths availability," writes Richard Swenson. My day-timer showed me that my family was getting the "leftovers of my life". When you keep track of the activities pulling on your time, you can assess what is out of whack.

- **Say yes, carefully.** Take a few days to think and pray before you commit to doing more. Our culture pushes us to feel value when you utter "I'm busy doing..."God encourages us to consult Him through prayer and solitude to listen to His wisdom. We are wise to rest and reflect.

Here is Phil Callaway's prayer to help us get our lives out of "Fast-Forward":

Heavenly Father,

Protect me from the distractions of a noisy culture, that I may hear your voice – and listen.

Keep me from giving too much of my time to those who won't cry at my funeral!

Grant me wisdom to separate the insignificant from the eternal opportunities that intersect my path a hundred times each day.

*Restore my body with your rest, season my words
with your grace.*

*Free me from the sin of comparison, the trap of equating
popularity with value.*

*May the days I have left be lived at your pace, as I greet the
success of others with joy, their pain with compassion, their
failures with grace.*

*And in the end, may I be remembered by only a few who
saw You reflected in me.*

Amen.

"FACING THE FALL"
AUGUST 1997

"We teach what we need to learn."
– Anonymous

This summer I've been reflecting on how I'm going to face the fall – harvest priorities, my needs, school-kids' schedules, and community expectations. I've written about the "Battle of Balancing" roles, and lectured on "Being Everything to Everybody". Frankly, I'm tired of being tired. So what am I going to do about facing this fall? I'm asking for input and advice.

My husband, full of common sense, suggests "decide what you want to do and be, and do a good job of it!" My problem is that I like to do all sorts of things. However, if I've learned to say "Yes!" I can also learn to say "No."

The process of balancing is never ending. Balance involves nurturing attention for the body, mind, and spirit. There is a saying, "Where there is too much, something is missing." I like the idea of making appointments with myself for fun time, friendship teas, and going for walks down the lane. Notice that I said "idea". I have to act !

Ellen Sue Stern, author of *Running on Empty Meditations for Indispensable Women,* says: "The compulsion to be super accomplished comes out of deep insecurity. No amount of achievement will make us feel loved. Loving ourselves comes from accepting our gifts and our limitations. When we define our identity through our achievements we limit and diminish ourselves. What we do is but a small part of who we are."

So what am I hoping to do and be this fall? I want to be a happy, healthy person. I want to nurture strong loving relationships with my husband, children and friends. I don't want to be tired, hurried and overwhelmed. I'll be writing some specific goals to hang on the fridge. I'm going to do it the 4-H way "learning to do by doing." My well is going to be filled with time to laugh at my writer's group, time to relax with books and artwork, and time for meditation and prayer.

Some of these thoughts may sound selfish. Those of us who have servant heart see many needs before us. Perhaps the "need is not the call". In other words, maybe I'm not the only person who can meet the need.　,

"When we insist on doing too much, we are not only inflicting the damage of this choice on ourselves, we are sharing this damage with those we love the most," Anne Wilson Shaef writes in *Meditations for Women Who Do Too Much*.

I like what actor Lily Tomlin said: "For fast acting relief – try slowing down."

"THE LOVE OF WORK"
AUGUST 1996

Our 7-year-old son is looking forward to selling $50 of sweet corn this summer. As he hoed his corn rows he asked me: "Mom, why did God have to make weeds? I hate hoeing!" I don't like it either, but the job has to be done. Corn seed matures in 60 to 78 days. How long we will work to grow "mature" kids?

Our challenge as responsible parents is to teach our children how to work at a task and stick with it. Children who do chores regularly become better problems solvers. Work habits and perseverance are modeled with action, time, good equipment and standards. Children like to know what is expected of them.

I've read of families playing singing games in the garden, or sharing stories as they work together. There needs to be a sense of accomplishment along with fun.

Check your attitudes towards work. Do you bound out of bed in the morning to do the important things, or are you caught in the lure of procrastination and chaos? Take time to give positive feedback and recognition with encouragement. Children need our presence – more than presents – in order to accomplish tasks.

Children are unique with different personalities. Firstborns may be the "doers" and high achievers while the family's baby may just want to coast. According to Bonnie Runyan McCullough and Susan Walker Monson, authors of *401 Ways to Get Kids to Work at Home,* the child needs to understand:

- your expectations of the job;
- advantages of doing the job, and the consequences if it is not done;
- the option the child has to choose between rewards or consequence;
- exactly which choice the parent prefers the child to make.

In *Pick up Your Socks and other Skills Growing Children Need* author Elizabeth Crary says "responsibility comes from understanding the task, accepting responsibility for the task and motivating one's self." Children who have good self-esteem, believing they are capable, responsible people find it easier to learn a task.

Motivating children with "we work first, then we play" is the approach Dr. Kevin Leman takes with chores for kids. Leman suggests: "Give your son responsibilities and simply tell him you expect them to be done. If he fails to follow through, then let the natural or logical consequences result in a loss of privileges. When using Reality Discipline use action, not words. Do no threatening, nagging, lecturing, or preaching. Simply take action and let your child learn from experience."

Family counselor David Irvine sees many clients who are suffering because they have never learned to be responsible. Irvine says he is thankful for all the opportunities for work he had growing up on the farm.

I want my children to see themselves as people who are capable of making a positive contribution to their family and the community. The hard part as a parent is to put Leman's tips consistently into practice:

- **Vary tasks.** Give kids new jobs and rotate responsibilities. Set time limits and involve the children in setting the timer.
- **Be a good example.** How tidy is your room? Lower your standards and accept less than perfect performance by your children.

Leman says, "What your children do is not a reflection of your personal worth, but it definitely is a reflection of theirs." Maximize constructive encouragement. The goal is to help kids grow and mature. Your motto is: "I will not do anything for my children that they can to for themselves." (That is hard to stick to!) The privilege to work is a gift, The power to work is a gift. And the love of work is success.

PONDER AND PLANT:

What do I need to start doing right now? _____

_____

_____

_____

What do I need to stop doing? _____

_____

_____

What do I need to share with my family and friends? _____

_____

_____

CHAPTER 3

FAMILY ISSUES

FAST TIMES … SLOW FOOD
APRIL 2001

"The snail is of slow motion, to educate us that being fast makes man inconsiderate and foolish." - Francesco Angelita

Recently, Brandon Chef Larry deVries was lamenting the fact that his cooking students rarely ate family meals together anymore, and their favourite desserts were Rice Krispie™ or puffed wheat cake that their grandmas made! Chef deVries spoke of the "slow food movement" which is gaining popularity with those who believe that time is possibly the most important ingredient in any meal. Slow food advocates want taste and pleasure at their tables, not the fast food culture.

"The family meal is being neglected in many hurried families," suggests Mavis McPhail of Manitoba Agriculture. People aren't making it a priority to share family mealtimes, but can you afford not to?

According to a task force on teen issues from Connecticut, keeping teens out of trouble boiled down to a simple and effective solution: the family meal.

Fighting against the obstacles of busy schedules and poor meal planning has big benefits!

The Connecticut group found:

- Children who ate an average of five meals each week with their families were better adjusted than those who ate an average of three. (Springtime seeding and autumn's harvest put great pressure on farm families, but occasional "tail gate" suppers and meals in the field can still be managed!)

- The socialization process when kids learn to define the ways in which they are going to live happens around the table. Table manners, taking turns speaking and listening, all add to everyone's social skills.

- Strong, healthy families communicate. Nurturing the soul of the family as well as physical needs comes with sharing the highs and lows of the family's day.

- Family meals give children a sense of security. One survey found that 2.5 per cent of the respondents never eat together! "If children wonder if they are going to be fed it makes it hard for them to take on other tasks. There is a relationship between love in a home (affection for one another) and the richness of the family table". Families who regularly gather around the table stick together and have more unity. For kids, that translates into the all-critical "group to belong to."

- Meals are one of the best times for tots to pick up new words. Kids whose families chat most during mealtimes have larger word inventories and are good readers.

- Eating with children teaches them healthy attitudes about trying new foods.

The important factor is to sit down together, not to eat a gourmet meal. Flexibility is the key; your microwave, crock-pot or "take-out" can help provide simpler meals. Encourage everyone to help cook, set the table and plan the next meal!

Sit down together and start together. In our family we say grace before the meal while we hold hands, thanking God for providing food and a place to be together as family. If shift work or team sports interfere, make adjustments by eating dessert together later.

No television or reading allowed! I can't believe that 50 per cent of American homes leave the TV blaring while eating...how rude! Many families now leave the answering machine on to catch phone calls. Our house hasn't mastered this yet as we run a home-based business.

Let everyone share and talk. Ask probing questions that require longer responses that just a grunt! Set a pleasant tone, and don't get too hung up on table manners, lead by example. Eating at the table facing each other enhances connecting. I prefer round tables set with linens and candles or garden flowers.

Don't rush. *"Ha, you haven't met my family!"* you are thinking. We all make choices every day that pile up into the big important beliefs of what is best for our family. Make sure that everyone is finished before anyone leaves the table without permission. Speedy eaters can linger, listen and participate.

As farmers we all work hard to put food on the table. Let's focus on building a stronger family by sharing many meals around the table together. It's worth the effort!

MENO-POSITIVE CHANGES
JANUARY 2000

"Aging is mind over matter, if you don't mind it doesn't matter." – Mark Twain

During the Christmas holidays, two things happened to help us on the road to better health. We moved our exercise equipment upstairs, and our siblings challenged us to get in better shape. Regular exercise helps keep my cholesterol level in check, and gives me more energy.

So how do I keep motivated to sweat? The clincher came when Dr. Mairi Burnett told her "menopause" audience that about one of every three women over 60 dies from a heart attack. It was one of those "Aha" moments when I realized my excess weight and exercise habits needed to change, now!

"Menopause is a bit like puberty in reverse" says Dr. Burnett, "the body is winding down." I like Debra Waterhouse's definition of menopause: "It is not a disease to be treated, but a transition to be experienced." Waterhouse wrote *Outsmarting the Midlife Fat Cell...Winning Weight Control Strategies for Women Over 35 to Stay Fit Through Menopause.* This was a practical, life-changing book for me.

Waterhouse is a dietician who encouraged me to take a "meno-positive" approach to my health. Here are some things to consider:

- **Attitude.** It is time to take better care of myself, and stop thinking about it. Living well is my goal, weighing priorities. Knowledge is power.

- **Fitness.** I'm focused on muscle gain not fat loss. I don't own a scale. Regular workouts and walks combat menopausal fat. Waterhouse says "your body will find its own healthy midlife weight."

- **Nutrition.** Eat smaller portions (about what will fit on my hand), and more frequent meals. "Eat well, eat less, and choose foods well," Burnett advises. No more dieting... ever! Farm women who eat their largest meal at noon are the smart ones – that's when our metabolism is most efficient.

- **Emotions.** "Physical hunger is when your body needs nourishment; emotional hunger is when your soul needs nourishment," states Waterhouse. She also gives whole-hearted approval to consuming chocolate as a menopausal mood stabilizer! "Outwitting stress is an effective way to outsmart midlife fat cells."

A group of farm women in Burnett's audience, were surprised when I confessed that I had missed the lesson that taught fat cells release estrogen. They were happily carrying their midlife weight and willing to discuss any menopause issues.

"Don't blame menopause for everything" advises A *Friend Indeed,* a bi-monthly newsletter on menopause (www.afriendindeed.ca). Become more informed about treatments, especially alternative therapies such as herbs. Dr. Burnett stresses that patients need to inform their doctors if they are experimenting with herbs. Beware of pills and potions with exaggerated claims and false promises. Don't believe that herbs will "cure" diseases, guarantee health or longevity. Herbs are rarely replacements for drugs, but options to supplement mainstream treatments, stresses Waterhouse.

The Mature Women's Health Program runs a Menopause Clinic; for answers to your questions call the Clinic at 1-204-975-7720. Use your library to gain more knowledge for making positive changes in your lifestyle. Don't wait for a heart attack to motivate you to be healthy. You can make active choices to be "meno-positive" today; you're never too old to change!

"GET TO KNOW YOUR MONEY… HONEY"
APRIL 1999

What is stopping women from taking control of their finances? "Fear! They don't think they know enough, and lack the confidence to ask for what they need," says financial planner Christine Smith.

Some women are hesitant to seek advice if they have little money, and others don't realize that financial planning is really talking about dreams, and how those dreams can be achieved. If you don't have a goal, how will you get there?"

What are the 3 most important things to address financially first?

1. **Financial goals:** don't be afraid to listen to your dreams.
2. **Know your "relationship to money".** One client was terrified to open her bills, and let them pile up. With Smith's help she addressed her debts, and is now able to plan to meet investment goals.
3. **Understand clearly the investment choices you have made.** Are they the right type of investment for what you want to achieve?

What does it cost to use a financial planner?
Smith says people in business should do what's best for their clients, and as an independent (no fee) financial advisor, she is

paid by commission. "If we do well for a client we get referred. Don't think you have to go to a paid advisor to get impartial advice. Look for someone who builds a relationship of mutual trust, respect, and who communicates well." There is no cost to clients unless they employ a fee-for-service advisor.

What are some hints for women to get their finances organized?

Gather all your financial documents to "really get to know" your situation before you meet with your advisor. Define your goals in terms of hopes and dreams.

Smith creates a written proposal which states assets and liabilities (net worth), goals, and the asset mix to achieve those goals. A yearly written review tracks progress towards goals. Rural clients can visit their advisor to maintain the personal relationship, and they keep in contact via phone, fax or email.

Here's a happy scenario of a woman who took financial action:

> *A couple came with a retirement dream to live in the Caribbean for six months, and six months at a cottage. They followed their plan diligently, setting aside certain amounts for 10 years. In 1998 they retired and started building a dream home, swinging their machetes on Cat Island saying: "We can't believe it we did it!"*

> *She says if she could say only one thing to encourage women to take control of their financial affairs it would be: "Face the fear and do it anyway. You can be free by taking charge of your life in every aspect by gaining a relationship with yourself and your money."*

Finances need to be faced, not avoided. Take a hard look at your relationship with your dollars. Get to know your money honey!

Empowering Teenage Girls
October 1999

A re you trying to raise a confident and assertive daughter, watching her struggle with great insecurity in junior high? You are not alone. The common advice to "just get her through it" doesn't seem very helpful.

I'm seeking positive ways to help children cope in a culture that worships airbrushed good looks in magazines, and sexual activity outside of marriage, while stifling the creative spirit and confidence of many teenagers.

I've wanted to write this column for a long time to encourage you as parents, grandparents, and friends. I urge you to mentor young women with practical affirmation and a ready ear to listen to their struggles. Mary Pipher, a therapist for teens, believes "what holds girls' lives in place is love and respect for their parents."

Pipher, who wrote *Reviving Ophelia: Saving the Selves of Adolescent Girls,* offers concrete suggestions for ways teenage girls can build and maintain a strong sense of self.

'We need to examine what it is in our culture that destroys the happiness of so many teenage girls. ... Daughters can learn to recognize the forces that shape them and make conscious choices about what they will and won't endure."

Pipher encourages these practical skills for teenage girls:

- Keep a journal or diary. Writing thoughts and feelings strengthens your sense of self. Young teens can use their journals for self-discovery.

- Smartness is not a liability, although many teenage girls "play dumb" to fit in. Define your deepest values and beliefs. Parents: talk to your teen about her passions, and what gives her life meaning.

- Find a place to relax, and focus on your thoughts and feelings for the day; then separate thinking from feeling. "How do you feel about this? What do you think about this?"

- Set boundaries of what is acceptable and make conscious choices to decide firmly what you will and will not do. Limits on time, bodies, companions, and activities are set. Teenagers choosing abortions when the sexual boundary was crossed anchor lifelong pain. You may not feel comfortable discussing these issues, but if you ignore the media's impact on your teen, you've got your head stuck in cultural quicksand!

- Define your relationships and learn to state your needs. Think about what kinds of relationships are in your best interest and structure your relationships in accord with your ideas. Talk about and make changes for positive teen friendships.

- Manage pain in positive ways such as exercise, reading, hobbies, prayer or playing the piano. Sports are a great outlet to meet physical needs, develop teamwork, and be successful.

- Volunteer to do good deeds for others helps; you'll feel good about your contributions, and become less self-absorbed.

- Homes that offer structure and affection with "I love you, but I have expectations" can help girls hold on to their true selves. Parents can help by listening to their daughters, who need as much time as toddlers, says Pipher. "Good parents manage to stay reasonably calm through the storms."

Depression in teenagers is sometimes not diagnosed by professionals who are reluctant to make that strong statement. Girls are vulnerable to depression if they are in an environment "where they are not validated" says Pipher. She asks a girl to record her personal victories and own validations so she is less vulnerable to the world's opinion.

I've worked with Grade 7 and Grade 8 girls for 15 years. Our daughter is now in high school. Don't just hide in the bottom of your family boat during the storm of junior high, set your course, and help that teenage girl find a strong sense of herself.

Focus on the Family has a great magazine for teen girls called "Brio" and one for boys called "Breakaway." Their resource to help you stay in tune with movies, TV, and music is called "Plugged In." Call 1-800-661-9800 to subscribe or ask for a sample copy.

You might think about a "coming of age ceremony" to celebrate your daughter's journey. A Boissevain family marked their daughter's twelfth birthday inviting women who were important to her. They were asked to bring modest gifts, bits of wisdom, and rituals that represented their own process of maturation, symbolic for the young woman.

It's time for all of us to care with compassion, to listen to teenage girls...and help them find a healthy sense of self.

CONNECTING

CHAPTER 4

DISCUSSING THE 'UNDISCUSSABULL'

"DISCUSSING THE UNDISCUSSABULL" JANUARY 2003

"The time has come – to talk of many things."
– Lewis Carroll

It was like there was a huge bull sitting in the middle of the living room, and no one in the family was willing to talk about it." In the peaks and valleys of life there are times when we know deep in our hearts that issues need to be discussed, yet the words get caught in our throats. Stuck. We don't like to show our feelings, or get stirred up with anxiety and anger, but our needs and wants beg to be put on the table. It is time to stop pretending that the "bull in the middle of the room" will go away on its own.

It is time to "discuss the undisscussabull" a new phrase I've coined to help farm families in the succession process face the tough issues directly.

What needs to be addressed?

Every farm family is unique, yet there are common themes of things pressing down on the transition decisions that need to be made. Here's a lengthy list:

- **Letting go.** These are loss issues. Can Dad build a new identity or role for himself beyond the farm? Is he changing his management role, or making a complete exit from the farm scene? Can Mom adapt to a new living space and plant more trees in a new yard? Will she still have access to the raspberry patch?

- **Retirement needs.** Many farmers forgot to plan for off-farm investments, so their retirement income needs to come from the farm business. Is there money for a new house or travel?

- **Dreams differ.** Does each person have shared goals and a vision of what the future should look like? A husband who dreams of a southern lifestyle may be linked to a wife who always wanted to stay close to the grandchildren!

- **Fairness.** What is your sense of tough justice for family who have helped for 20 years on the farm and those who found careers outside the farm? Is fairness based on need? The neediest one gets more, so fairness is achieved when the neediest reaches the level of the other kids. Is fairness based on equality, where each child gets an equal amount? Or is fairness based on equity, determined by contributions? The person who contributed the most, gets the most.

- **Keeping the farm intact.** Your century farm holds a lot of history. Is there guilt associated with even thinking about selling your grandparents' legacy? How viable is the farm to cash flow the support of two families or more?

- **Work styles.** Who needs to take a holiday? Do you mutually agree upon goals for this farm? How do workaholics and leisure lovers work together? When Dad retires, will you let him drive the combine?

- **Family goodwill, also known as relational capital.** This is the really big, big issue. "I just want my family to get along. I want peace." Do you know how to give each family the space needed? Are the opinions of the "in-laws" welcome at family councils? Do you practice forgiveness?

- **Business arrangements.** Who has power and control in the decision making? Is there a plan for profit sharing?

What contingencies are there for the death of the founder or successor? Is there more than one successor? Do you need to think about expansion?

- **Direct communication.** Are you listening intently? Can others trust you to respect and understand their feelings and wants? Can you find a healthy way to deal with conflict at family meetings?

- **Entitlement.** You inherited a lot from your parents. Do your children feel they are "entitled" to an inheritance? Separate bequests, gifts, and family issues from the business issues of ownership, wages, and profits.

- **Pre-marital agreements.** Divorce is a huge "undiscussabull." Does the family need to protect the farm business from a marriage breakdown? How do you build trust when you demand pre-nuptial agreements?

- **Resolving conflict.** Are many of your family arguments historical? Do pride and stubbornness keep the bull in the middle of the room?

- **"AAA Club".** Abuse, alcohol, anger. Your mental well-being rides on taking self responsibility for making healthy choices, and necessary changes.

The things on this list that are hard to talk about are called "the soft issues of succession."

As a farm family coach, my conflict resolution studies have given me a great appreciation for facilitators willing to help committed families work carefully at "discussing the undiscussabull" in a safe, respectful forum. Grab the bull by the horns, reflect on what you need to talk about and keep listening to the needs, wants, hopes and dreams of your farm family. Conflict is part of life. Choose to move the bull out of the living room. May there be peace in your pastures and parlour.

How to Deal with Conflict
March 2003

In any relationship, conflict is normal. Yet, how a family resolves fights is a curious thing. Here are some of the variables in "fighting fair".

Attitudes toward conflict

- **the avoidance approach:** "If we never talk about it… maybe it will melt away like snow." Then blizzards come! Stuffing unresolved issues and hurts usually deepens the intensity of the pain.

- **the accommodating approach:** "Well, what would make you feel better dear?" The people-pleaser side of you makes sure others get what they want, but you forget to ask for what you need to see a problem solved.

- **the compromising approach:** neither party is happy with the outcome, but they bite their tongue and try to live with it.

- **the "me" approach:** focuses on competition where the conflict involves getting one's way without much consideration for saving the relationship.

- **the "collaborating" approach (I encourage this one):** you talk about the issues, are highly committed to resolving the problem, and come to an understanding and agreement about being "hard on the problem, but soft on the person."

Conflict management styles vary with the people involved, and the family habits they bring to the scenario. I come from a family where raised voices meant you should be listening more closely. The directness of my parents' communication rubbed off on me, as I tend to be a bit more direct than those who prefer a subtle approach, like "I was wondering if you had noticed that this was happening…"

Then there are those complete ostrich types who don't want to get involved in the hot situation at all, so they stay away, are not engaged, and suddenly have to go do chores or fix something.

Communication styles can be a huge conflict bump for your family. Introverts want time to process your information: engage brain before speaking. Extroverts use language to process thoughts and ideas while speaking. Body language speaks volumes also. Asking for a style of communication that works for you is tough, but the results are worth it. Have you checked out what "OK" really means as a response? Is it "yes" or "I hear you but I don't necessarily agree with you?"

1) **Attitudes towards disclosure.** "In some cultures it's not proper to be frank about emotions, about the reason behind a conflict or a misunderstanding. People differ in what they feel comfortable revealing," according to Mediation Services trainers who teach a course entitled Culture and Conflict. (Call 204-925-3410). Questions that seem natural to you, such as "What was your role in the conflict?" may seem prying or meddling to others.

2) **Future versus present versus past orientation.** Some arguments tend to get historical and hysterical. Past-oriented people are concerned about traditional values and ways of doing things; they are slow to change. If you're truly goal oriented, and you want to ask tough questions to get to the heart of the matter, your future orientation will collide with people who relish the past, and don't like to see things change too quickly.

3) **Decision making styles.** Does your farm family bow to the wishes of the patriarch, or is it egalitarian – everyone gets equal input towards making decisions? We all have a deep need to be appreciated and not be taken for granted. If conflict rears its head due to lack of consensus, do a reality check on the best way to make decisions. Does your family delegate, rule by majority or look for consensus?

What's your communication value orientation? My value in communicating through conflict is definitely focused on relationships, and teamwork motivations. I'm a PEOPLE person. ACTION people value getting things done, solving problems and achieving goals. PROCESS people like things to be organized and follow a structure or a plan. Then we mix it up with the IDEA people who see the big picture, with creativity and innovation. Families where all children have completely different personalities can create problems. We all need to recognize the bias we bring with our perspective and values about how communication should happen when we are fighting an issue.

Farm families would be wise to evaluate which value each individual holds: people, action, process or ideas. Then the team can understand how each person may have a different slant on what the problem is, and the best way to work towards resolution.

Men and women also see things differently. Gender differences in how we talk about issues have been explored in Deborah Tannen's book, *You Just Don't Understand.*

Men are looking for information, so their talk is of a reporting nature. Women are looking for interaction, so they want to establish rapport.

Dealing with conflict is not always pleasant, but avoiding conflict is death. Farm families that really want to learn more positive communication skills, identify the real issues, and generate solutions are to be commended for their courage and perseverance.

Learning about conflict resolution builds understanding and in dealing with the tough stuff that is part of our lives. Make an appointment with yourself today; learn to deal with family conflict with skill.

TEN TOOLS FOR TALKING ABOUT TOUGH ISSUES
MARCH 2004

My childhood experiences chasing steers have come back to encourage me to use the "bull" metaphor for helping families discuss the "undiscussabull"…the tough issues.

Here are my top 10 tools for getting communication flowing:

1. **Take charge, grab the bull by the horns.** This is about taking responsibility for changing yourself. Only you can change you. Life is full of stresses, challenges and change, but we decide if we grow through the process. You have to deal with conflict in a timely fashion, and not let it fester. You have greater options for resolving conflict or misunderstandings if you deal with them soon!

2. **Come from curiosity.** Curiosity in communicating well is about not being judgemental or finishing other's sentences. It means using the statement "I'm curious how you see it, or tell me more about what you expect." Seek out common ground, things you both want to see happen, and use the word "I" instead of "you". I feel … I need … I want … completing the blanks. If you point fingers and say "you always" or "you never", defensiveness sets in to kill the conversation.

3. **Ask deeply.** You can be soft on the person, but hard on the problem. Probe with open-ended questions, those that can't be answered with a simple yes or no. Balance the speaking and listening time. Frame your questions with descriptions of your own feelings and intentions.

4. **Play with possibility.** I use a Beanie Baby ox as a talking stick for family meetings. Whoever is holding the ox gets to talk without interruption. Possibility means employing the upward spiral of positive thinking and comments that help create solutions and map out dreams.

5. **REALLY LISTEN.** "When I listen, people talk." You can build understanding by checking out assumptions. Try not to interrupt. Use the ebb and flow of your talks to focus on the key message. Paraphrase what you heard, and check it out with the speaker to see if you are on track. If you have been tuning out your family, you know the consequences. You remain stuck.

6. **Ponder and percolate, not prod.** Bulls aren't keen on being prodded, and neither are people. We need time to digest,

sift, and give ourselves space and time to think. If you have tough issues to process, have a conversation, and then give yourself some time to sleep on the ideas presented. Letting new options perk for a few days is a good idea. While you are pondering, consider the other person's perspective .Ask gently, "Is there anything else ?"

7. **Cultivate trust.** Bulls aren't likely to charge those who have built up their trust in the feed pen. When you "walk your talk" and treat family with respect, you can build confidence in the relationship. If the emotional climate is unsettled, you may have to intentionally work on building up positive emotions before you can establish new levels of trust. People "don't want what you want" when they don't understand your idea, they have a negative emotional reaction or they don't trust you.

8. **Respect boundaries.** As kids we were keen to know how to reach the fence before the stampede of steers. I have scars from barbed wire, when we cut things a little fine.

   Are you conversing with your son as his father, or his boss? What expectation of roles is clear to you, but not clear to your listener? Are there some tough issues that you just agree to disagree on? Boundaries involve setting guidelines for respectful communication, and honouring confidentiality.

9. **We all end up in a box ... cardboard or coffin.** We know that someday we will die. Coming to terms with your life and how you want it to be involves dealing with your loves ones. You need to face the aging process, you will not live on this earth forever. Reconsider your future, and let your family know your intentions! Talking about your will and funeral plans is tough, but necessary!

10. **Extend the olive branch.** We can all use our words and actions to be peace makers. You can create the legacy of open communication and healthy relationships by practicing forgiveness and telling your family how you love and appreciate them. As soon as bull riders remove the strap on

the bull's haunches, things settle down. What ways can you make peace and harmony happen in your farm family? Is it up to you to take the first step and model a forgiving spirit and attitude? Ultimately, you will have to pass on your authority, so practice letting go with seeking forgiveness.

WHO WANTS THE FARM?
MAY 2001

"Ignoring your passion is like dying a slow death."
– Cheryl Richardson, author of *Life Makeovers*

For more than 16 years my friend and colleague, Donna Hastings, has been listening to farmers talk about hoping one of their children would take over the farm or wondering how they were going to talk their child out of wanting to farm! Which is it for you?

Who is going to run the farm? The plan for succession to the next generation lingers on the minds of many farm families. Unfortunately, there is a huge group of farm families who are really stuck – letting their pride, ego, or neglectful attitudes stop them from finding out "Who wants the Farm?"

A recent show on "passion" hit home for me. They weren't talking about sex, they were encouraging people to really find out what they love to do and pursue that. Do you still have a passion for farming? Do you think one of your kids might have a passion to continue the family business? Have you ever bothered to openly ask your family what passions and goals they have?

If you were to die soon, what would you regret not doing? Hastings asked her audience of outstanding farmers these questions:

- Why do you stay farming? Or why did you come back to the farm?

- Why did you start farming?

- What would you miss the most if you couldn't farm?

May is typically the time we honour our mothers and ultimately show respect for our family relationships. If your family farm is multi-generational there is a lot of pride involved in continuing the family farm tradition. Many believe agriculture is a great way of life and the best way to raise a family, even thriving in the hard times of rain, drought and low prices. The passions of the older generation mixed with patience and dedication have helped families achieve success.

How can you change the attitudes in your family? Ask! Family communication barriers need to come tumbling down and quick!

- Brainstorm with your friends and others to call upon their wisdom in overcoming the obstacles. Talk to people you admire and copy their successes.

- Network by building your own dream team of people who can show you options.

What would you be doing right now if you were not afraid of what people thought of you? Long-time farmers are packing up, selling land and moving to a new province to be closer to their children. They are doing what they feel is best for their family and not living up to the neighbour's expectations.

- Find a mentor who can help you focus on your passion and main goals.

- Find encouragers to strengthen your support system. Who are the people who can support your passion emotionally, physically or with information?

- Face your fears about breaking down the communication walls with the family and take action! Do you really want things to stay the way they are?

I married a farmer 20 years ago. Today, he and I still share the passion to farm and wonder if our children will carry on 20 years from now. While you're waiting for the fertilizer tank to fill, take some time to reflect on "who wants the farm?" May you have no regrets in following your passion.

TRAITS OF SUCCESSFUL FARM FAMILIES

- Talk about what you love about farming, share your passions and communicate!
- Give children real responsibilities early on to learn good decision making as you let go.
- Teach children how to manage money temptations and delay gratification.
- Encourage children to learn from others; maybe by leaving the farm for a few years to work for someone else.
- Dream and allow others to dream. Who is on your dream team? We all need to be highly motivated to farm.
- Balance work, family and community. Relationships are your biggest investment.
- Separate the family from business, and have fun together!
- Appreciate each other's uniqueness, and show appreciation.
- "Don't sweat the small stuff."
- Teach your children the love of land.

Is the Farm Terminally Ill?
September 2003

I was deeply touched and saddened as I read Karen Emilson's diary of a cattle producer in a farm paper. Honestly, how do you encourage a farm couple who is feeling crushed against a political wall with huge bills to pay?

What do you want when your farm feels like it is terminally ill? Hope. Hope that you will find a way to make things work again. Where is a sense of hope when you feel like your farm is dying?

As a believer, my hope is in God, that He will make a way. As an encourager, I ask you to ponder and consider how to process and live with bad news and blocked borders. As a farmer, I've learned to separate the things I have control over and the things I don't. Glean from the learning of people with terminal illness, and see if some of their wisdom can transfer to the farm that feels like it is terminally ill.

"Be aware that bad news is always bad news, even if it is given in a respectful, compassionate manner. No one wants to hear that they themselves or a loved one is dying," says Dr. David Kuhl, author of *What the Dying Want*. Dr. Kuhl's 10 years of research compiles practical wisdom for the end of life using the stories of terminally ill patients. His chapter headings can be touch points for farm families who don't want to see themselves as victims, but who are looking for opportunities to cope with the current crush of anxiety:

- **Time and Anxiety:** "Anxiety can be reduced by introducing certainty," Kuhl says. He encourages a plan for care and a life review. What plans do you have to continue to take care of yourself, physically, emotionally, spiritually, and financially? There is no certainty when the blocked border will open. Embrace the attitude that you will seek support from one another, neighbours and friends. Now is not the time to be fiercely independent. Communicate with your creditors. It is okay to ask for help. If you're a grain farmer, visit your cattle farming neighbour.

- **Being Touched, Being in Touch.** High stress sometimes causes people to physically pull away, when the best thing might be a hug or a handshake, and a phone call. In the words of Frederick Buechner, "Whatever else we are, we are bodies and that as bodies we need to touch and be touched by each other as much as we need to laugh and cry, and play, and talk, and work with each other."

- **Speaking the Truth.** People have a hard time talking about imminent death. Telling my father that mom was never coming home again wasn't easy, but it had to be done. When I met a cattle producer acquaintance this summer at the beach she said "we're still in denial". How can you be truthful with your family when you aren't even sure where the farm is at? Start by calling a family meeting. Let everyone have a chance to speak, listen, and flow with the conversation. If you are a "family who doesn't talk," call someone in to help facilitate the meeting. Visiting a dying relative is always better done sooner rather than later. Talking about the impact of the farm's financial scenario is best done today, with farming and non-farming family members.

- **Who am I? You call yourself a farmer.** That's what you do for a living. Who are you as a human being? Is the farm your life? When a severe crisis hits, many things come into question. Tell your story to a trusted listener, or call the farm stress line. No one chooses to have financial failures. Your goal is to keep your personal integrity through a very tough time. Your cash flow has been crunched, but you can choose not to compromise your character.

- **Transcendence – the spiritual dimension.** One of Kuhl's co-researchers found great comfort in the slogan "Let go and let God." This slogan is easy to say and difficult to follow says Dr. Kuhl. Feelings of grief come with a deep sense of loss – loss of income, loss of energy and loss of hope for the future. Life on the farm with heat, grasshoppers, and hungry stock is very hard, yet I sense my pastor would encourage us to read about Job's trials and still trust God.

The BSE experience showed a deep need for farmers to feel connected to the urban dwellers who eat the food. Paycheque people don't understand how 30 cattle can be your entire cash flow. Being in touch with non-farm family and friends may help you feel emotionally supported, but ultimately someone needs to carry the cause to bring home the severity of the farm's terminal illness.

Continue talking things out with family, friends and financial players. Find people who understand what farming really means to you. Consider your character, integrity and what really gives your life meaning. Pray for God's strength and wisdom. Play with your grandchildren. Read Kuhl's book.

PONDER AND PLANT:

Take a few index cards and write one word on each card that describes a tough issue or conflict that you need to talk about. These "undiscussabull" cards are like flash cards that you can place on the coffee table, and literally put your issues on the table for discussion.

MY UNDISCUSSABULLS ARE:

_____

_____

_____

_____

_____

_____

_____

_____

_____

_____

_____

_____

_____

_____

_____

_____

_____

TEAMWORK

WHAT MAKES STRONG FARM TEAMS?
MARCH 2004

"The most effective way to achieve right relations with any living thing is to look for the best in it, and then help that best into the fullest expression." – Allen J. Boone

Today, one of the most frequently asked questions by farmers is: "What can I do to make better use of the labour in my operation?" Farmers can increase the "horsepower" in their businesses by harnessing the skills of all family members. Are you overlooking the valuable input of your spouse and children by leaving them out of major decisions? Non-family employees have valuable insight, too!

Here are six essential elements for building a successful farm team:

1. **Pick partners who get along.** I often have coaching clients request some assessment of whether the "brothers will get along". Spouses and farming children need to have opportunities to take responsibility, be creative, and make decisions based on mutual trust and respect. Strong families have a loving interaction style that is courteous and kind. Father/son relationships are respectful and patient. Conflicts are managed as they arise. Strong families take

pains to clear up difficulties quickly so that the problem is attacked – not the person.

2. **Clear goals and long-term commitments.** Not knowing when Dad is going to let go drives families crazy. Not knowing the long-term commitment of sons and labourers to work hard drives Dad round the bend. Successful farm families have a legacy of innovation because they are inquisitive and open-minded. Their innovative attitude pays attention to detail, quality, marketing, sound financial decisions, self-discipline, solid work habits, and great problem solving. Does your farm have job descriptions and performance appraisals?

3. **Growth for everyone.** To move business forward farmers need to ensure that all team members learn new skills and cultivate their special talents. It helps to know the personality styles, strengths and weaknesses of everyone involved. Accepting people's differences without judging helps encourage clear areas of designated responsibility, and work which receives recognition and respect. Parents are wise to support higher education, special training, and skill development that goes well beyond what they may have in a particular farming area. Profit-sharing with family and employees is a tangible reward system for the team.

4. **"When I listen, people talk."** Effective communication is the foundation of business growth. Confident communicating families can bring up problems, talk them through, and arrive at mutually satisfying solutions. Good listening habits and respectful expressions of opinion are essential for problem solving and negotiations. Slamming doors, looking at the ground, and swallowing your anger will destroy the team. Successful farm business meetings help families plan for change and solve conflicts. When is your next business meeting?

5. **Respectful social distance.** "I don't want to talk about farming at family gatherings." Families need to have fun together without tensions or control issues. "In-laws"

should be accepted for who they are, with their needs and opinions considered. Each family should enjoy minimal intrusion from other family members on how they live apart from the business. Each family unit needs clear boundaries and its own sense of autonomy.

6. **A plan for the next chapter.** A strong farm team faces the issues of transition and succession as a process. Parents are more willing to let go of management if they have other interests and lifestyle choices outside of the farm business that are enticing and rewarding. There are lots of emotional issues affecting the planning process which all employees and family need to address. Strong business teams know that future financial security and viability will be maintained by the next generation of managers.

Recipes for failure:

- Failure to have systematic business communications.
- Unresolved conflicts that add stress and tension to daily living.
- Lack of incorporating the younger generation into significant decision making.
- Intrusive and controlling management styles that cause hurt, resentment and anger.
- Poor communication with anger and disrespect, and an inability to solve problems.

Great traits for success:

- Build your enthusiasm by reading and surfing the internet for new ideas.
- Use farm meetings as research and networking opportunities.
- Make innovation your top priority.
- Take a vacation, get a new perspective and be refreshed.
- Search out better ideas and ways of doing things.

- Be a self-starter, only you can change you…get going!
- See problems as opportunities to meet new challenges and make good decisions.
- Be assertive, and pro-active about taking more risk.
- Open your mind to new possibilities.
- Be achievement oriented rather than security oriented.

Why are the "soft issues" (such as human resources) so tough? A farm business is typically quite independent, sometimes with little public interaction or small appreciation for interdependent thinking. Some farmers don't learn to bridle their tempers or govern their emotions in the workplace. Many people just don't see conflict management as a priority, they blow off steam or hide their anger, rather than finding out how to solve the issues at hand.

Pride is a huge factor in agriculture. By making progress or "doing it alone", any success or prestige is reflected back on the farmer. "When farmers put work ahead of the family's or employee's well-being, they can become quite self-centred and demanding. They think they are "right" and take a forceful, intimidating way of making their points, shutting others down in the process," according to psychologist Dr. Val Farmer. Farmers have a hard time of letting go of the work. When management is top-down, they don't let others have a stake in the outcome - financially or emotionally.

"He who has the gold makes the rules." Farmers with this attitude can use their right as landowners and ultimate decision-makers to bypass the ideas and needs of others on the farm team. Those who have power, can sometimes abuse power.

Being a manager of people on a farm team takes work to develop listening skills. Unlike the farm pickup, it is not automatic! Many people are poor listeners. It takes a certain mindset to seek to understand other's needs. Some people are poor at giving positive feedback, recognition and constructive criticism. Others are poorly organized and make business decisions haphazardly.

What make a strong farm family team? A team that keeps work and family life in perspective. They strive for happy marriages, motivated and committed successors, shared management, good communication, and delegation. They use outside expertise to improve the business, and ask for input and advice.

MEET TO MAKE THINGS HAPPEN
APRIL 2004

Why do you need to meet to make things happen with your farm team?

Answering the "why" before the "how" will build a strong case for change. People need to know why something is important before they will commit to the process. Many decisions need to be made and communicated fully to everyone trying to get the crop in, feed livestock, or manage the forages. Many families tell me they just haven't gotten around to having family business meetings on a regular basis, and especially not during the busy season.

Wait. Who said the meetings needed to be long? Plans fail or get mucked up when people don't know how to talk through problems and solve issues together. Meetings reduce stress, even short 15-minute Monday morning meetings before the week gets rolling.

Conversations over the dinner table don't cut it especially when several families farm together. Formalized family business meetings are important because they help members separate personalities and emotions from the business decisions that must be made. Meetings also build support for major change.

How do you make it happen? You need some structure. Select a chairperson, follow an agenda, set down rules of conduct, and take minutes. The first rule for a successful meeting is that everyone be there. All team members need to show up. If you had a part in solving an issue, you'll work harder at making it happen. Meetings provide a forum for planning. Most people are happier with decisions they've help make rather than decisions that have been forced on them. People can find many creative ways to stop you in your tracks if you don't build a case for decision making with everyone's input.

These people need to be at the meeting:

- Those who understand what is going on.
- The people with power to make decisions.
- The family members who have to take action to carry out the decisions. Founders, this is the chance to groom your successor and teach decision making skills to the next generation!
- Those people affected by the decisions taken.

Establish an agenda. Agendas keep everyone on track. Use a clipboard or bulletin board to collect important items to be discussed. Make sure the agenda is self-explanatory... "we have cash-flow crunches ahead, what are our priorities?" Prepare to come to the meeting with a good attitude and the facts needed to choose the best solutions.

Guidelines for good meetings:

- No shouting, no personal attacks, and an agreement that it's okay to get angry and leave the meeting for a five-minute break, but you have to come back. Only one person speaks at a time, each person is given time to speak; and each person speaks only for himself. Find common ground to work from.

- Have a chairperson to keep a good tone to the meeting and the discussion on track. Start and end the meeting on time. Encourage everyone to speak up and, as the leader, reserve your comments until all others have spoken. Define problems in terms of issues, not personalities. There are two sides to every issue.

- Beware of expressing your own opinions too early if you are the boss. Ask probing questions like "Is there anything else?" Shut cell phones off to avoid interruptions. Have someone record the issues discussed, the decision made, who is to act, and by when. Every decision made by the group should have a name for action attached to it.

- Document long-term policy issues like holidays and strategic business plans separately from the weekly business meetings.

- Write things down, so everyone can refresh their memory in the future! Notes symbolize the business nature of the meeting.

What do you have to do to get farm business meetings to happen at your place? Talk about it, but you have to take action! If your family needs help in managing conflict, find an outside person to help you talk and fight fairly. Conflict is normal, arguing is okay, but resolution needs to happen. Meal time conversations are not typically recorded, and how decisions are made is important to remember for future reference!

Find a good location to meet without interruption. If different family members are responsible for different enterprises or divisions, let them report about their area of concern and responsibility. The family team is like a board of directors with suggestions and approval for the business decisions made.

What's the plan for this week? Seeding is hectic, but every day we start by making sure all workers know what the plan is for the next few days. Things change, but communicating directly and clearly keeps things going smoothly. If your family team is bursting with frustration because too many important decisions are being made "on the fly "then it is time to be intentional about a formal business meeting for effective problem solving to make things happen!

DIARY OF A WORKAHOLIC
MARCH 2003

Sometimes the overwhelming nature of farm demands causes the entire body to slump at the kitchen table. Worn hands stroke greying hair and the eyes are reddened and glassy. Farming is one of those unique places where you live at your workplace. The line between work and home becomes blurred. It seems that work is always just out the back door. Working too much is killing the farmer and his family. People with a work addiction see their "jobs as an escape, and find it difficult to be emotionally present to their families" says Dr. Bryan Robinson, author of *Chained to the Desk...a guidebook for Workaholics, their partners, and children, and the clinicians who treat them.*"

Many farm families push really hard in calving season, seeding, haying and harvest...but the healthy families take time to renew, rest, recreate and have fun. Workaholics follow self-imposed demands, cannot regulate their work habits, and just don't know how to have fun with their family, because they are overindulged in their work.

Farm men tend to wake up one day in their late 50s and realize that they haven't really developed any hobbies. They know how to work, they know that work consumes them...but as the markers for retirement approach (whatever that means) they have forgotten to have fun with their families. Work addiction "masquerades as a positive addiction" says Robinson. The hard working farmer is praised for always being in the field at sunrise, and working 16-hour days. He is deemed "a really hard-working guy" who provides for his family. Did anyone ask the family members if Dad was present for special parties, Sunday afternoon fun, or a child's hockey game?

Men and women alike need to assess if they have supports built into their family habits to prevent workaholism from taking root. Here's Robinson's Reality Check:

1. The source of work addiction is inside us. Workaholics are not team players, they need to control, and cannot

delegate. Dad's inability to let go and always work is his choice.

2. Workaholics create stress and burnout for themselves, and fellow workers. You may have clear boundaries about taking time off, or having breaks, but someone else on your farm is pushing you to keep going, when taking pause would actually increase everyone's productivity.

3. Workaholics operate from a "Messiah Myth" that says they have to do it all and save the company. They believe the myth that they are superheroes, wedded to their farms. They actually have poor self-worth, difficulty with intimacy, and fear of loss of control.

4. Workaholics overextend themselves to fill an inner void, to medicate emotional pain, and to repress a range of emotions. They tend to work just for the sake of working. If your loved one can't turn off the cell phone, or live with checking the email just twice a day, then technology is enabling the addiction.

5. The release of adrenaline creates physiological changes that lead to a "work high" that becomes addictive. I wonder if this is the "High of Harvest" which is followed by weeks of needing deep rest when the rush is over.

6. You don't need a job to qualify as having a work addiction; maybe you are a "careaholic." You are burning out as a caregiver of others, and meeting the needs of others without taking care of yourself.

7. Workers who live balanced lives are more efficient and productive. They bring greater quality to the job because they are less stressed and more clear-minded.

Recovery requires some deep processing of the source of the pain coming from the inside of the person. There is boundary setting and time management to be done. Take work lightly and play seriously. Are you trying to fill a void of loneliness that has its roots in your childhood experience?

Workaholics are always in a rush and hyper busy according to Robinson. Control is the name of the game. Nothing is every perfect: "if you want it done right, do it yourself" is their motto.

Farm family relationships crumble when pressed overtime by grumpy work addicted farmers. Work is done in binges, not researched properly, and sometimes impractical.

Workaholics think they are only as good as their last project as their self esteem tanks are running on empty. Performance is how they measure their worth.

"The best predictor of a positive approach to work, is a full life outside of work," says Robinson. For farm families that means taking time each day to find a healthy pace, and anticipate fun and fellowship away from the fencelines.

Complete these phrases:

- *I do a lot of …*
- *Because it makes me feel …*
- *And helps hide my fear of …*
- *The source of my beliefs come from …*

"Workaholic farmers are lazy at relationships," says psychologist Dr. Val Farmer. Read *Chained to the Desk* and discover ways to support your family's healing from work addiction. Your family needs you to be present and to celebrate with them. Your farm business will thrive when the manager lives a balanced life. Retirement will not be a dirty word, when you've intentionally taken time out to create hobbies and have fun.

"DAD, LET GO!"
FEBRUARY 1997

"If it is possible, so far as it depends on you, live peaceably with all." – Romans 12:18

Let go Dad!" addresses the issue of the farming father-in-law fuelled by readers responses to "getting along with mothers-in-law."

The process of transferring the farm to the next generation eventually hits the withdrawal stage for the parent couple. Sadly, this stage is sometimes left to be dealt with in the will, rather than in progressive changes when all family members can talk about dreams, decisions and expectations face to face.

The process of "letting go" for parents can be gracious. "It means we deliberately let go so each of us can grow and learn on our own. For most of us, letting others go is neither natural nor easy. The thought of letting them fail, or fall, is extremely painful to us," says author Chuck Swindoll in *Grace Awakening.*

In the life cycle of the farm you might try testing your child's commitment with wages. The next stage may be some purchases of assets for your farming children. Once well established you may encourage the child to buy into the business. Then the withdrawal stage hits when the parents start to leave before the farm is completely transferred. Let's address some areas to practice "letting go":

- **decision making** – Hopefully management decisions have been made jointly, and now you are ready to say to your child "You decide." Struggles to have some say in decisions are likely a big area of conflict especially if he is now 40!

- **land** – The pride and security of ownership is a hot spot of dissent in multi-generational farms. Your identity as a farmer is not tied to what you own, but who you are. Changing title of the home farm before death, and transferring title immediately, even if Mom and Dad hold the mortgage, is a big part of letting go.

- **presence** – Your help around the farm is really appreciated in your transition years Dad, but sometimes a little privacy would be nice. Get away from the farm to a neutral place to talk about separating family and farm business issues. Work on those hobbies and community friendships, too!

- **advice** – Farmers tend to have an independent streak, but letting the farm go graciously and financially begs the use of professionals. When transferring the farm, a lot of emotions come into play. Rather than take out emotions on siblings or parents, work with professionals, who can help loosen the reins with objective perspective.

- **bad attitudes** – Let go of those negative attitudes towards change. I know you like things just the way they are, but accept and embrace change. "Know that not all change is good. Maintain balance and perspective. Stay connected with people," encourages David Irvine, a seasoned farm transfer counsellor.

- **manipulation** – Scrap your need to control others. Express your needs and wants, but use good listening skills to hear and understand the dreams of other farm players.

- **hard feelings** – Let go of hard feelings towards the younger generation or the "in laws." Forgiveness therapy is the hot new counselling strategy of the 90s. Own up to failure by saying: " I'm wrong, I'm sorry. Will you please forgive me?" If a person chooses to forgive, they will experience release.

- **small things** – Overlook small things, keep the big picture of family harmony in mind. The ability to let go of small things is a trait of successful farm families.

Release your grip on the farm Dad, if it is time to start letting go. Hang this poem up in the shop, or tuck it at your bedside. The author is unknown but the words are powerful.

Letting Go

To let go doesn't mean to stop caring,
it means I can't do it for someone else.
To let go is not to cut myself off
it's the realization that I can't control another.
To let go is not to enable,
but to allow learning from natural consequences
To let go is to admit powerlessness,
which means the outcome is not in my hands.
To let go is not to try to change or blame another,
I can only change myself
To let go is not to care for,
but to care about.

To let go is not to fix,
but to be supportive
To let go is not to judge,
but to allow another to be a human being
To let go is not to be in the middle arranging all the outcomes,
but to allow others to effect their own outcomes.
To let go is not to be protective,
it is to permit another to face reality
To let go is not to deny,
but to accept.
To let go is not to nag, scold, or argue,
but to search out my own shortcomings and to correct them
To let go is not to adjust everything to my desires, but to
take each day as it comes
To let go is not to criticize and regulate anyone, but to
try to become what dream I can be
To let go is not to regret the past, but to grow and live
for the future.
To let go is to fear less and love more!

GOODBYE HOME FARM, HELLO NEW MEMORIES
MARCH 2004

C limbing a large rock pile and checking the chicken coop are two fond memories of my childhood playtimes in Grandma's farm yard. Farm families have a hard time saying goodbye to the memories held with the "home place." Letting someone else take over the yard, or selling out, evoke tears and a deep sense of loss in some folks.

The loss is about the change of ownership and control that raises the question: "Where are my roots now? Where is my sense of place?" The sadness comes with a loss of connection to your family of origin and wondering if the new owners will respect your need to visit now and again.

In our farming culture, we have rituals like auctions sales, fall suppers, and fairs to mark certain seasons or events. I think it is time to create some traditions that work for families to mark transition and change in moving from the home place, with positive actions. I'll call it talk, walk, and mark.

- **TALK.** Avoid the "nobody asked me" syndrome. This typically happens to the non-farming children, usually girls, who aren't invited into the farm family discussions about the future of the home place. Tears may be mixed with the talking, but that's okay. Share feelings and expectations about how to honour childhood memories, and a deep connection to the home yard. The next generation may want access to share the sledding hill, walk in the bush, or skate on the dugout, even if the property has been transferred to a sibling or new owner.

- **WALK.** My senior friend, Peter was taking a walk down memory lane by showing his new wife the farmyards he had lived on. He found a lateral branch that he had bent 60 years ago to make a frame for a play tent for his younger sister. The branch was fixed by the growth of the tree, and he was amazed by the memories that flooded back! Walking around the yard as a family or gathering for a picnic can create a special sense of connection. Our siblings dashed through the snow in our backyard at Christmas, and re-lived the fun of the tire swing, forts, and a game of fox and geese. If you are selling to new owners outside of the family, you might like to get permission to walk the property in the future.

- **MARK.** Someone once said that the best time to plant a tree is 20 years ago. On our yard special trees mark the death of my sister, my mom, and my father-in-law. Yet a large Scotch pine also marks the date of our marriage. Trees are symbolic growing markers of special times. My mom planted a black walnut the summer she died, and she said she was happy knowing that I would enjoy it when I was 90! When we levelled a vacated yard site, I asked for three large cottonwoods to be spared as a marker of "Primrose Farm". These trees are a curiosity to the neighbours, but I don't mind them being called "Elaine's trees."

You might want to keep a scrapbook of memories of the home place. Use a digital camera to capture your fondest images, and mount them on foam core board inside an old window frame. Weld a sign that recognizes the date of the homestead with the family name. Collect horse shoes, rocks or farm tools that will remind you of your roots.

We sent a digital photo of a large photo of the farm circa 1960 to be re-produced by an artist on a cream can for our urban sister. She was thrilled to have a keepsake of her family home. Quilts with special pieces and sacred stitches can also capture the family's ties to their childhood home.

Saying goodbye to the home farm can be done in a myriad of ways. Help the person grieving the loss find a special way to keep a connection to their roots. If a garden full of flowers is about to be destroyed, call family members first to see if there are garden treasures that can be transplanted. Save pieces of barn board for special framing projects. Photograph special sites or objects before they are sold or ploughed under. I am fortunate that I can visit my childhood farm home and have tea with my dad. I entertain my husband's family at the home they were raised in. I have to view my Grandma's rock pile from a distance, as a stranger now owns that yard.

Find ways to talk about, walk about and mark the special connections you have to your home farm, especially if you are preparing to say goodbye.

PONDER AND PLANT:

What are the things that you need to let go of that would make your family and/or team stronger? _____

_____

_____

_____

CHAPTER 6

PLANNING FOR CHANGE

HOLD ON, TAKE ON OR MOVE ON?
CONCEPTS OF THE HUDSON INSTITUTE OF SANTA BARBARA
NOVEMBER 2003

"Change is inevitable, growth is optional!" – Anonymous

In November we take time for remembering. We recall the hard won freedom of our country and tuck the fields in for their winter's solitude. I encourage you to take time to reflect on the life lessons of the past farming season. Be courageous. Are there things you need to hold on to, let go, take on, or move on?

This process is not just a memory jolt. Taking a hard look at the changes you've experienced this past year will give you a clear idea of where you might be headed.

- **HOLD ON:** What things are you doing that you want to continue? If farming is your passion and you want to hold on to the farm business, what does that look like to you? Describe what a really great day on the farm would look like. Can you express your desires to your mate? The business is one aspect of your life, but what family activities are a high priority for you now? The support of family and friends can help you survive the storms of farm life. Studies have shown that rural women withstand the stress of low income and long hours of work provided that they have a supportive spousal relationship. How well are you holding on to each other?

- **LET GO:** Sometimes we need to conduct minor surgery on our lives and fix what hasn't been working. This might mean being really honest about what our addictions have been costing our family and business. Are you addicted to work, food, alcohol? Do you care too much about others at the expense of your own well being? If you are feeling stuck in your current situation, you might want to create an exit plan. Making the transition out of your current work role on the farm may mean working different hours or only working when you choose to come and help out. The whole process of letting go is difficult. The BSE fiasco has shown us how a lack of control of markets can devastate an industry. Can you let go of the things that are out of your control, and focus on what you can change?

- **TAKE ON:** I'm a firm believer in life-long learning. I want to take on projects that will help me be a better person, relate to others, and help our family and farm business. The farming lifestyle can be fulfilling when you feel what you are doing is meaningful. What things would be good for you to take on this winter? Are there some new skills you need to learn? Is it time to face your mortality and work on a plan to transfer the farm? Is it time to have more fun and find out where the old-time dances are scheduled? Is it time to learn how to work the wood lathe, and dust off the books waiting to be savoured?

- **MOVE ON:** What season of life are you in? The forties have different challenges than the fifties, sixties and beyond. You may not want to "act your age", but ask yourself what challenges you expect to meet at your stage in life. Forty-year-olds want to take charge. The fifty crew focuses on the quality of their living, and lightening the stuff they carry along. Age 65 is not a marker of being old, but when the brown envelope is a regular item in the mailbox, one might ask "What does 'starting over' mean to you?" Some people choose not to retire. Those farmers over 70 may want to move on with mentoring the next generation and leaving a legacy.

Love the age you are! Life is a grand adventure, more like a "Slinky" than a straight line. Perhaps you just want to get on with your life, and not change very much. The years slip quickly by, and so may some of your dreams if you don't stop to reflect on who you want to be and what you want to do. I'm a human being first, wanting to be intentional about caring for myself, my family and my community. Character really counts.

Planning for change may sound impossible, but dig down and figure out how you want to restructure your current scenario. Farm families are resilient and can draw on many resources. You can choose to cruise through the winter doing things the way you've always done, or you can look at your situation with courage and say "some things around here have to change."

Planning for change involves:

• Holding on to what is good and right for you.

• Letting go of the habits, activities, and roles that don't work for you anymore.

• Taking on new learning projects, and unlearning things that keep you stuck.

• Moving on with a timeline to accomplish what your life stage requires of you.

Farmers are famous for living in "next year country." My challenge to you is to learn from the past year's trials. Take good care of yourself and your family – physically, emotionally and spiritually. Find a quiet place to contemplate what you want to hold on to, what needs to be let go, and new things to take on. Then move on … ready for the next challenge.

READY, SET, GOALS!
MARCH 2002

It happened to me again this morning, the woman on the phone said "Oh, Elaine, you sound busy!" My response was, "I don't really like that word. I'd rather call it being intentional about what's important to me."

In our community, small groups of farm couples are starting to gather on a regular basis to talk about their quality of life. They're setting new priorities for people, land, and profit. As you are reading this, take Joan Bond's advice and write down 10 things that are extremely important to you.

Writing things down turns dreams into goals. Thinking is hard work, but the reward is having a clear picture in your mind, and on paper, about what is really important.

Steven Covey writes in *First Things First* the idea of "putting the big rocks in first" into the jar of your life. If you know what is important – things like planning and relationships – then you will enjoy the quality of life you are seeking. You'll be less likely to waste time with trivia, T.V. or running from crisis to crisis.

Here's what my list looks like. It is taped to the front cover of my day timer.

> LOVE ... from God and family
> MY HUSBAND ... healthy relationship and vital partnership
> KIDS ... growing, godly, skilled
> HEALTH ... losing weight, walking
> REST and BALANCE ... getting a good sleep, journaling, being thankful
> SHARING ... faith and fellowship with friends.
> LEARNING ... reading new ideas, being creative
> ENCOURAGING ... through speaking and writing
> TRAVEL ... adventure, seeing old friends
> FORGIVENESS ... letting go, making choices

Your points may not be perfectly clear, but keep jotting. What kind of quality of life is important to you? Who do you want to spend time with? Where do you want to put your energy? What hobbies or passions have you been neglecting? What kinds of things do you want to say "YES!" to?

I did this exercise with a group of rural women. It dawned on some of them, that they were frustrated because their current activities had little to do with what was down on their list. Our farming lives have different seasons of intensity, but the list tells us what we cherish and value giving us direction in the decisions or choices we make with our time.

Have you ever considered beginning a list of your life ambitions or dreams? Seventy-year-old John Goddard wrote a list of 127 life goals when he was 15. Many of them were challenging, like climbing the world's mountains, running a five minute mile, and reading an entire encyclopaedia. He's completed 107 or more of his goals!

Take some time to make a dream list. Write rapidly without editing about everything that you would like to achieve in the next ten years. Consider all of your life, the physical, emotional, mental, spiritual, educational, and financial. Next step: Write the numbers 1,3,5,10 or "C" beside each item on your dream list. (1 means that this goal is important to you in the next year, 3 = three years, 5 = five years, 10 = ten years, and C = continuous).

Congratulations! You now have a written list of goals with a timeline. Farm family coach David Irvine says, "The purpose of goals is to entice you to become the person it takes to achieve them. It is the *journey* that is important, not the destination." Clarifying your life's goals and priorities helps you to focus your energy. It also gives you a map to monitor life decisions.

That's what I mean about being intentional. There are lots of interesting things to do, but what kind of person do I want to be, and what am I called to do? Some people are so frantic with handling day-to-day problems, that they have never stopped long enough to determine if they might be able to make better choices that line up with what they really do value.

Don't wait for cancer or a heart attack to push you to reflection. Privately ponder what you hope to be and do. Share your thoughts and plans with those you love. Enjoy the success of living a high quality of life on your farm, or ranch, that fulfils you.

What we want to do is work smarter not harder. If your passion is to touch lives and make a difference, get out your road map of goals. Successful people write things down. You'll be amazed at the results of writing down your goals to help you enjoy a better quality of life.

STRETCHING OUT OF YOUR COMFORT ZONE AT 50
FEBRUARY 2002

Farm succession is a serious issue, but when push comes to shove, only about 18 per cent of the farm families in a 1999 Ontario study had an up-to-date legal will. Only 2 per cent had fully developed succession plan. Are we in denial?

The joint study, by the University of Guelph and OMAFRA, asked advisors to identify the issues that often created problems. Family issues topped the list of barriers. The advisors suggested that farmers should start early and determine a few different equitable options. Once the process was started, and options identified, the farm family could consider tax implications. Advisors noted that in most instances, farm families did the opposite, they focused on options and solutions to minimize tax liabilities and ignored the family issues.

"What is the farmer going to do with himself?" is a question that is "outside of Joe's comfort zone, so he just doesn't go there," says financial planner Duane Davidson.

In your fifties you need to name your fear and deal with the urgent issues of what retirement and farm transfer looks like to you. Do you fear:

- Family conflict?
- Loss of control?
- Loss of wealth?
- All of the above?!

"Family conflict is to be avoided at all costs." This type of thinking that conflict avoidance is a virtue, is like being diagnosed with high blood pressure and refusing to treat it. Everything is going to explode. Frank, honest family discussions of everyone's expectations is what the estate doctor prescribes. Your adult son is now home from agriculture college, he's educated with lots of other career options. A two-year "testing period" with wages or profit sharing will show you if you really can work together.

Communication is a key skill at every age! For some great encouragement go to www.farmsuccession.com.

What are your control issues at 50? Who is responsible for the management, production and marketing decisions? Are you less tolerant to risk as you age, or can you see re-organizing the business with a good father-son agreement? Decisions in the next 10-year horizon are critical, as time flies by you have fewer options. In the Ontario study, the older generation "just couldn't let go."

Fear of not having enough to live on during retirement or loss of wealth is real. Unfortunately, having all your retirement fund come from only farm assets threatens the viability of the farm. The inability of the farm to generate adequate cash flow to feed two families and ensure a comfortable retirement becomes clear when you get real tangible numbers in place. When you set a figure and do lifestyle planning for your retirement, you need to track family living expenses for a few years to avoid surprises and shortfalls. Now is the time to benchmark your future income needs from the operation and look at how that is going to be funded. At 50, you still have some flexibility to maximize your off-farm investments. You can also check different business structures like family trusts and freezing the estate. You need to seek out the costs and benefits of insurance as a tool for cash for the next-generation, or as a payout to non-farming children.

Alberta Agriculture has a simple six-step succession plan:

1. Discover expectations. Get everyone talking and sharing about their yearly, five-year and 10-year goals.

2. Explore options. At 50, you still have options.

3. Build a succession plan.

4. Check with the experts.

5. Finalize the plan.

6. Implement the plan. Someone once said, "It takes 11 times more energy and effort to implement the plan than it does to design it!"

Feeling frisky at 50? Good! You have a lot of work ahead of you. Face your fears, and get out of your comfort zone. It's time to make some hard decisions if you want a happy family as your legacy.

WHEN PUSH COMES TO SHOVE
FEBRUARY 2002

I met a farmer at Ag. Days who was having trouble with a certain engine. He said after months of frustration it was great to meet a guy at a display that solved his problem in two minutes. The company engine representative's focus on the external source of fuel was not the problem, it was internal valve adjustments that were needed.

A lot of farm families wish their estate concerns were as easy to fix as engines, but transferring the farm business is a time for tough decisions. There are internal issues (the people problems) and external factors (viability of the farm business). If you're in your sixties, you've now reached an urgent stage for planning. Refusing to make any decisions is a decision, and you may be feeling "push is starting to feel like shove!"

Why do families feel the shove?

- **We don't know to whom or where to go for help.** Getting expert advice for converting your assets into future income is only a phone call away. Choosing advisors takes careful research. Talk with your team of farm business professionals and trusted family or friends for referrals. In Manitoba, we have a great team of extension staff at your local Ag. office.

- **Avoidance.** At 60, do you think you are immortal and indispensable? Avoiding thinking about making plans for the future is deciding to stick your head in the sand. How healthy are you Dad? Can we talk about labour issues, too? Living wills and health issues need to be discussed.

- **The problem is too complicated.** As the old adage says, you can only eat an elephant one bite at a time. Start by listing the 10 most important things to you in your life. Goals will energize you, and give your life purpose and meaning. Talk to financial professionals about your investments, crop insurance, minimizing tax etc. This can be done in stages, but the most important thing is to implement your plan. Have deadlines for your goals.

- **Parents are too stressed out.** At 60, you may be caring for an aging parent or just plain tired of the stress of keeping the farm afloat! Managing your stress by making plans for your family's future may seem like a hard pill to swallow, but the estate doctor recommends treatment before you expire!

- **Dad is a control freak!** If Dad is being deliberately vague and indecisive about farm transfer plans he is trying to control the behaviour of the farm children. Fear of losing control is a big issue even when many workable options exist to let Dad make the transition gradually. Remember that succession doesn't have to mean severance.

- **"Hanging on."** Society has marked age 65 as the magic age of retirement, even when some active, healthy people are still going strong farming in their seventies. Not planning to retire is a reason to avoid estate planning, unless you have exciting goals to anticipate. "People who are not good at retirement planning aren't good at estate planning either," says psychologist and farm family counsellor Dr. Val Farmer. (www.valfarmer.com)

- **Families are afraid that succession discussion would create conflicts.** "Harmony now, disharmony later" is a motto some families adopt, which means the family avoids asking each child what they want and lets the will solve the issue. Dr. Farmer recommends: "Have an open reading of the will with everyone present. Be prepared to explain the plan and be open to suggestions. If they hear it from their parent's lips, children will accept there was no undue influence."

- **Deciding what is fair is a tough call.** The farm is a business, not a legacy. Fair does not mean equal if you have made a decision to leave the core assets of the farm intact. Assets are not love. Honour commitments. It is a tragedy when the farm is split up to be "equal." Chartered Accountant, Alyson Kennedy also advises parents to set a price for selling to children and stick to it. "Once the number is on the table you can't go back and change it. People make plans based on the number given."

Gentle pushes for transition:

- **Better communication.** Eighty per cent of effective communication is attentive listening. Can you clearly describe what you need? Be open about your frustrations, even if it causes some discomfort. "It is better to push the dialogue so that important issues are talked about. Use courtesy and tact to ease defensiveness," says Dr. Farmer.

- **Take a break.** Let the younger generation prove their worth to gain trust and confidence. If the farm is well looked after while you're on holiday or away, you can learn to hand things over gradually. Developing interests away from the farm will make retirement more appealing.

- **Have family meetings.** Practice an open, democratic style of decision-making. Agree to disagree if some issues are seen from different angles. Your farming children may have different goals than you do.

- **Let your children shine with their specialty.** One couple appreciated the computer and marketing skills their children brought to the operation. People need to feel appreciated for their contributions.

Farm viability, retirement needs and goals, fairness to children, lifestyle dreams – are all things to "fix" in your estate plan. Take a good look at your internal pressures and problems. Don't let push come to shove. Take time to make plans. Go for it!

The Vintage Advantage:
What to do at 62, 72, 82, and 92!
July 2004

"We are all happier in many ways when we are old than when we are young. The young sow wild oats. The old grow sage." – Winston Churchill

What is most on the mind of a farmer who is about to leave his farm, or let someone else manage? I have a strong hunch that many farmers do not want to talk about life after farming because they don't have a hot clue about what they will do in the future.

"Vintage advantage" is a term coined in a focus group about redefining retirement. A coaching group was brainstorming about what looms large in the minds of elders as they seek new meaning for life after work. Can you see advantages as you grow older?

Age 62 seems to be a special age. That's when clients face their fears and call me for coaching, since 65 is only three years away, and that's when society says you are supposed to retire. WRONG! Some farmers will never retire, they will just die in the dirt, and that suits them just fine.

At age 72, when you can concentrate on your legacy and being of service, you might still be in fine shape to drive the tractor and help out. You might also want to stay home to work in the body shop, wood shop or coffee shop!

At age 82, you likely can count on living to be 100. My mother-in-law is this age, and she has to reschedule her visits to the farm because she has work to do taking care of "the old people."

All of us should plan to live to be 100. Have you noticed that people are living longer? If you are "retired" at 65, you likely have a good 30 years of living left!

OH MAN, OH MAN, WHAT WILL I DO? Exactly.

- **Find good role models, 10 years older than you are.**
  Check out the farmers in your neighbourhood who have
  found great things to be and do besides being farmers. In
  our town you could join the re-cycling crew twice a week,
  help build a local daycare, plant flowers for the town, host
  at the campsites, work at the hardware or convenience
  store, or help out local farmers during seeding and harvest.

- **Re-invent yourself.** Focus on what you really value and
  cherish. Think big, not small. What kinds of things give
  you energy? We have farm folks who help the poor rebuild
  homes during the winter season. It makes them grateful for
  their living spaces when they return home in the spring!
  Another farm couple has found meaning in helping out
  camping ministries down south, and locally.

- **What would a fun day look like?** Most farmers can't
  imagine what a day off the farm would look like. They
  don't garden, golf or go south, so what are they to do? July
  is the perfect month to start experimenting with fun. When
  the haying is done, and before the winter wheat needs
  combining, check out some fun activities. Dust off the
  camper, and book some time away from the farm to gain
  new perspective. Check out a new part of the country or
  visit the city relatives or your children. Enjoy the family
  and the outdoors. Cruise the Internet for creative strategies
  or clip the farm magazines for fun ideas. Play with a new
  hobby!

- **Be aware of your sadness, but anticipate joy.** Making a
  graceful exit from being a full-time farmer is important, but
  so is creating a new beginning for the next chapter of your
  life. I look at the transition as a type of "lifetime harvest".
  You've worked very hard for a long time. You've never seen
  a hearse pulling a U-haul, so maybe it is time to spend
  some time and money on you! Financial worries may be
  pulling you down, but talk to a certified financial planner,
  and talk to your children about expectations. You're expecting to live for a few more decades, and you can prepare as
  best you can for that reality.

- **Measure time differently.** Relationships make you rich. Good ones are a treasure. If you are ready to take your life off of fast-forward and push the pause button, make a conscious effort to evaluate how you want to spend your time. Test out new ways of doing things gradually. I have a friend who routinely goes to Victoria for a month every March. She is testing out a new lifestyle, and still is grounded with family responsibilities.

- **Nurture your servant heart.** Retirement has to be purposeful and giving. I have a senior friend who is a wonderful serving man. He helps build houses for Habitat for Humanity and loves the latest reno project at his daughter's house. When we serve others, we are nurturing the spirit and soul that God has created in us. You might want to tackle a grain drive for your community or other projects. Maybe you'll join the next overseas tour to find out what you can do to help a third world country.

- **Be healthy.**

Read *The Virtues of Aging* by Jimmy Carter. I'm looking for a new word to describe life after farming, because retirement doesn't really appeal to many farm folks. The Carters have discovered that there is a full life after peanut farming, and the presidency.

I love to travel, and it's genetic. My 78-year-old father did a farm tour to Brazil in 2004, he is active on the farm, and he still can dance up a storm on the weekends.

I hope you'll be intentional about exploring new ways to find meaning in your daily activities. Your identity is not tied up what you do for a living. Make a meaningful life as you enjoy your "vintage advantage."

PONDER AND PLANT:

Take 10 minutes to write down the 10 most important things in your life...

Now, what's your plan?

_____

_____

_____

_____

_____

_____

_____

_____

_____

_____

_____

_____

_____

_____

_____

_____

_____

CHAPTER 7

HARMONY

DAUGHTER-IN-LAW HARMONY
OCTOBER 1996

"For this reason a man shall leave father and mother and cleave to his wife." – Genesis 2:24

I've been a farm daughter-in-law for 15 years, in harmony with my mother-in-law. My dictionary defines harmony as "the state of being harmonious, free from dissent or ill feeling." Sure, we've have had different viewpoints or feelings on farm family issues, but overall we both want to get along. I've learned that I can only change myself and I'm responsible for my own happiness.

I've counselled families in the transfer process, and listened to the pain of families losing their farms A common theme is "I wish they would treat me like an adult, and listen to my dreams and feelings for a change." How well are you listening?

When I married, my husband and I left our families of origin and made a new independent family. Part of being a new family is figuring out the rules and expectations that have governed the family you left, but travel with you to your marriage.

Expectations affect our reactions to relationships. I am a "hugger" and "feeler" who married a reluctant hugger. Over the years I have learned to affirm my mother-in-law with hugs, especially in tough times. Meaningful touch can bless others and create harmony. Express your needs and wants. "I need a hug!" Greet each other graciously. I decided to call my mother-in-law "Mom," as it felt right, and we were intertwined with the farm business. Our first meeting in my home economics offce led me to help her choose wallpaper and carpet for her renovations. Little did I know that two years later I would be married to her only son, and living with that wallpaper!

Speaking of "the house," here are some contentious issues and how I've dealt with them:

- **The home.** My husband has lived in our house since he was four. It legally became our home (with title) 12 years after marriage. Only then did we feel real freedom to renovate and make permanent changes. There is lots of emotional attachment to the family farm home, but mothers-in-law can let go of this and freely encourage change without resentment. This is a useful phrase: "It's great to see you take such good care of this place. I'm happy you can make improvements."

- **Garden and yard.** Weeds are not a certified seed grower's friend. I do my best but my standards differ from my mother-in-law. We put in the garden together every spring, which is the annual rite of family history storytellings as we plunk in corn. I often thank Mom for the shelterbelt I enjoy as fruit of her labour 30 years ago. The peer pressure among young farm women to have a garden is something you may have to let go. Choose what works best for your family, maybe a smaller garden or none!

- **Food.** Harvest meals were once the sole domain of Mom when I worked off the farm. I appreciated her help and didn't feel guilty about her involvment. Today she still drops off wonderful baking and goodies to help me out. I choose to accept these as tokens of love, not judgment that I'm not feeding my family well. We choose our response; I choose to be thankful and positive.

- **Kids.** Grandparents have wisdom in child rearing. They also give lots of clues to "family rules" by how they speak to your children. In-laws, respect the wishes of parents if a child is not to have more ice-cream or treats. Talk sensitively about helpful things you've experienced to support the daughter-in-law's parenting style.

- **Finances.** Our attitude towards debt is greatly different from our parents who survived the Depression. We acknowledge this and talk about it. When the farm transfer took place, family meetings with a professional kept everyone's emotional bank account in good shape. If you're a mother-in-law who feels "it's awful the way she (daughter-in-law) spends money," remember your son is involved, too!

- **Holidays.** Here, there are differing values. How many hours should family members work? I'm reminded of the cranky daughter-in-law who finally was relieved after nine years that her father-in-law stopped waking them at 5 a.m.! Our family value of having Sunday as a day of rest has built better family relationships.

- **The Future.** In my books, farm women are farm partners. The issue of transfering the farm to the next generation needs lots of discussion with outside professional expertise and good listening to everyone's hopes and dreams. Share decision making and power. Don't assume anything ! Our accountant helped us ask hard questions such as: "What would you plan to do with the farm if your husband died?"

Learn to verbalize your feelings. Describe up-front what you feel by saying "I feel ...when ... because ..." Using "I" messages conveys the thought without making the other person feel defensive. Learn to say "I'm sorry."

My farming friends have shared hurts about relationships with their in-laws, but not a lot of positive experiences. We tend to share the negative and keep the good things to ourselves. If we could grasp the truth of Exodus 20:12, "Honour your father and mother so that you may live long in the land the Lord your God is giving you," we all may enjoy more farm family harmony.

How do we treat the girls?
March 2004

*"He who has bread has many problems.
He who has no bread has only one problem."*
– Old Byzantine Proverb

As a farm family business coach, I haven't found much written about the ways girls are treated in succession planning, but I have had lots of vibrant conversations. The culture around the will and estate expectations has changed significantly since the 1930s.

"We all knew the farm would go to the boys. We were born in the '30s and everyone expected Dad and Mom to roll it over to their sons. We were given educations, no land."

"We wondered why my sister and I were not part of the family discussion about who would have the home place. It really hurt. Dad couldn't understand why I was crying, when we talked about it later."

"The girls in our family all married well. I guess our parents felt we were well taken care of. My brothers got all the dairy quota and the farm. We girls got $10,000. I'm not sure my lawyer today would think that was fair!"

"Out here in dry land Saskatchewan we wonder if we're lucky we got cash and we are not stuck with the risk of the farm!"

"We sisters each got one quarter of land before our parents died, even though we don't farm. It was part of how our parents defined fairness, as all the siblings always got the same dollar support. Our farming brother was able to buy land from us and we gladly held the mortgage."

"In our family we don't fight about any inheritance, because our parents have nothing.

It's great. We all get along and we have fun together. The girls have good educations and can make their own way."

"Dad taught us all how to be skilled on the farm. We had no brothers! He treated us with respect and I think it makes him happy to see one daughter actively farming with her husband and our father."

Today, adult children are not happy with the "nobody asked me syndrome." This is where families keep decision making a big secret, and only the farming adults are involved in conversations about the future of the farm business.

I don't know the statistics on how many people read their wills to their children, but I do know that, according to a survey a few years ago, one in five Ontario farmers didn't bother having a will. Today, people are encouraged to discuss estate plans openly.

Each family must come to terms with what works for them. But my motivation to write this column comes from a common theme that exiting farmers are asking: "How do we treat the girls?"

So girls, gals, women, ladies! What are your expectations? Here are some of the comments I have heard:

"We want our parents to enjoy their hard earned finances during their retirement and aging years. We want mom and dad to have some fun for a change!"

"We expect good health care in place for Mom and Dad, so we want to make sure there is money available to have them cared for. I don't want to be the primary care-giver for my parents, I have a husband and children to look after already!"

"I accept anything my parents choose to give me as a bonus. They have already helped me get a university education and raised me in a loving happy home. I am proud to make my own way and will finance my own dreams."

"I'm glad to know that the BANK OF DAD is still open, but realistically, I need to build up my credit rating. It's nice knowing there is some financial support available from my parents if a crisis hits, but I need to do things on my own. I'm the daughter who got the farm. Some days with the tight cash flow I don't know if that is a blessing. The investment cash my sisters got looks pretty good right now."

Every family has unique challenges and goals. In most cases, it is the farming sons that take over the family farm. Each family needs to talk about what the needs, feelings and wants are for the next generation of farmers. Avoid the "nobody asked me syndrome" and have a full conversation with the entire family group. Find creative ways to treat everyone well in the succession process.

WHAT DOES FAIRNESS LOOK LIKE TO YOU? MARCH 2003

One of the hardest conversations a parent has with a grown-up child is: "What do you expect from me as your inheritance?" I bet there are thousands of families who can't find the courage to put this question on the table, let alone think about it.

The issue of fairness is a multi-coloured monster in many farm families. Some have gone to court over it, some have internalized their frustration and broken off family relations, and some have let it go.

What does fairness look like to you? This is a general, open-ended question. In some families, fairness is having each child, regardless of financial circumstance, receive equal amounts of cash or support from the parents. When you survey the family history, you're likely to find a parent who suffered great unfairness in their family of origin, and has vowed not to let that happen to the next generation. I have witnessed the scenario where all the siblings of a family were treated with equality, which was judged to be fair to all. Some will argue that you cannot be fair and equal at the same time. In these families fairness is seen as helping the adult children who are the neediest financially. "We'll help out Charles and his family, but Chris is doing fine on her own with her family." Chris is not acknowledged as needing even basic appreciation or attention from her family of origin. Be careful not to make assumptions. A gesture of kindness, and checking in with your adult children as to how they feel appreciated as family members is a key conversation to have! An inheritance of thoughtful appreciation and love is more valuable than cash!

Fairness in some families is about rewarding those who contribute the most sweat equity and time to the farm business. That child is deemed to be the one who won the family competition for the inheritance of the business. "Deciding what is fair is a tough call. It takes a huge amount of assets to farm and the return on investment is paper thin. The farm is a business, not a legacy," writes Dr. Val Farmer, who counsels farm families. The on-farm heirs may want to inherit the farm as a gift for their years of hard work, labour, and sacrifice. Did you pause to ask the non-farm heirs what non-farm assets may make up their gift? This is the toughest issue to talk about, because in the busyness of making a living on the farm, many farmers forgot to create some cash flow that was not dependent on what happened at the farm ... if there are no non-farm investments or insurance, parents feel strapped in being fair to all their children.

Some farming children see fairness as paying Mom and Dad the fair market value of the farm business. They take pride in managing the risk and mortgages that the parents may hold in their retirement. They don't want anyone to think that they "were given everything."

Competition and sibling rivalry that is not discussed is a recipe for disaster in family relationships. Grab the bull by the horns, and reflect on these thoughts: What is my concept of fairness? Am I responding to or reacting to the way I was treated as a child and sibling? Who is going to open up the family discussion about fairness? What kinds of non-monetary gifts have we shared with our family to show our love and appreciation? That includes things such as time, child care, acts of service and helping out.

Remember to consider your own needs as aging parents. Your children may want you to keep more assets for your own benefit, and they may feel the love and nurturing you've already given them is the best inheritance they will ever receive.

What Do We Owe Our Kids?
February 2004

One of the toughest things to talk about openly in the farm business is how do we treat our children with our assets? Donna Hastings heads up the Canadian Association of Farm Advisors (www.cafanet.com), a group of professionals who are committed to high quality advisory service to farm families. I've added some of my farm family coaching experiences to Hasting's tips:

1. **In theory you don't owe your children anything.** You gave them life, education, love your values and your vision. It's amazing what young adults will tell their parents about this when they are asked directly. I have heard children say, "Dad and Mom, please enjoy yourself for once, enjoy what you've worked for all your life. I don't expect any money from you now!"

2. **Put your thoughts on paper** to be able to reflect on these ideas and scrap the ones that don't seem to work. Move slowly on these decisions. Think of it as a work in progress...knowing each draft gets you closer to the finished product. Writing things down doesn't cast them in stone, but it gives you a perspective to re-visit and ponder. I recommend using a binder that holds all the planning papers from the accountant, financial planner, broker, lawyer, etc. This way you have a portable collection to keep your planning process organized, and see gaps or questions that need answers.

3. **Make sure that both spouses more or less agree** with each other before the children are brought into the discussion. You want to avoid pressuring one parent against the values or choices of the other. Don't set dollar values on assets for sale unless you intend to stick by them. Changing prices and changing expectations mid-stream creates a lack of trust.

4. **You both want to do the right thing.** Your children also have some ideas about what you or the farm owes them.

Your ideas and your children's ideas may not agree, but, remember, it is your estate and you built it. Ultimately, you make the decisions about who gets what and when. Also,consider that you will likely live another 20 or 30 years and need a good retirement income!

5. **Consider the wishes of the children.** Ask them to write a letter indicating what part of the farm, family heirlooms or non-farm estate interests them. Ultimately, it is not what each person wants but what each person can live with that will solve this puzzle.

6. **Ask yourself, "Why do I want to give this to this child?"** Doing the right thing can be tricky. Don't do it if it is because you feel guilty or want to correct a wrong or fix something that happened in the past.

7. **Tell your children what you are considering.** The feedback you get will give you valuable direction in "tweaking" the final draft.

8. **Don't keep it a secret.** Once you know what you are giving the children, to charity and to your retirement ... tell the kids while you are still alive to explain why you did it the way you did. It could save a lot of heartache, unanswered questions and hard feelings after you are gone. Keeping wills secret is not a good thing. In today's culture, the families who communicate their intent openly will be leaving a greater legacy of understanding with their family.

9. **If you are giving away heirlooms, or any items, make sure the family history goes along with it.** It will mean more to the new owner and help instill a sense of belonging.

10. **Ask other farm family business owners what they think they owe their children.** Listen to their rationale. Read. Consult outside advisors to ask the difficult questions to move the parents and the children along.

As the Chinese adage says "talk does not cook rice." Talking is a good place to start, but ultimately we have to act on our intentions. I realize that some of you may be 55-year- old children who don't know what your mother's will says, and also have 30-year-old kids who want to know what the next plan for your farm business is! Call me at 1-866-848-8311 with your excuse for not moving forward with these tough issues, or send an e-mail to elaine@elainefroese.com. For more information go to www.cafanet.com or find an advisor to help your family make decisions. We all know enough sad stories, it's time to write a new script.

PONDER AND PLANT:

Write a letter about your expectations for inheritance. It won't kill you. It may save a lot of hurt and heartache down the road.

Use this outline to guide your children's thoughts on paper:

Dear Mom and Dad,

I am very grateful for everything you have already provided me with.

I am especially thankful that you _____

My biggest hope for the transfer of your estate is that _____

_____

These are some of the memories tied to things that you own, that I would like to keep as a reminder of our family. Family heirlooms:

_____

_____

Just stuff that's important to me: _____

_____

_____

Farm assets or property: _____

_____

Non-farm estate items: _____

_____

_____

_____

I would also like us to find a way to plant a special tree, make a scrapbook, or take a special photo of the farm. Something to mark this new chapter in our lives.

Thanks for your most priceless gift, your love.

Signed: _____

Date :_____

My goal is to have things written down by _____(date).

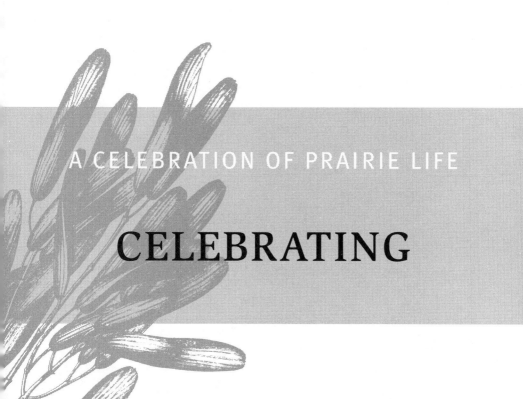

CELEBRATING

CHAPTER 8

LOVE

WRITE A LOVE LETTER TODAY
FEBRUARY 1999

"Love is patient. Love is kind." – 1 Corinthians 13

I don't know what to get my wife," the farmer lamented. I'd shared lunch with a group of farmers and suggested that a love letter would be the perfect gift. But no one thought they could do it!

Valentine's Day is the perfect opportunity to make loving memories. Do it on paper. Getting a frying pan is not romantic! Opening a carefully chosen card or reading a hand-written love letter is a blessing that lasts. If words don't come easily, get to the card shop now and spend some time finding a great message.

Home-made cards are wonderful. You can compose a poem or verse for your loved one, or write a short note entitled, "This is what you mean to me."

Years ago, my father carved a birch bark heart poem for my mom, and that framed note of love withstood the test of time on their wall. It was an encouragement to our family to express love openly. My dad learned from his father, Bruce. We have a collection of love letters and poetry my grandfather wrote to grandmother when they were courting in the 1920s. The love letters are a lovely window on a relationship before my time.

When I was updating my day timer, I carefully transferred one of my husband's love notes. I relish these words on the days when things don't go right. You might use a bright pink file or special wooden box in your office to retrieve some "warm fuzzies" from people who expressed care for you in words.

A Valentine's Day treasure hunt is fun for families with youngsters. Shirley Dobson in *Let's Make a Memory* suggests:

- Buy a package of inexpensive children's Valentines.

- Write a different love note on each of 10-15 cards, or write one word per card to form a message of love.

- Hide the cards throughout the house or in the car.

- Give a written clue on the outside of each envelope, directing your "Valentine" to the next card.

- Include a small "love gift" with the last valentine. Tucking notes of love in lunch bags, briefcases, work boots or suit pockets is fun.

Our daughter tried to buy a friend's Adidas bag but my friend explained, "You don't sell memories." The Adidas bag had been purchased in Indonesia where the family had spent three happy years. You sell cattle, land, seed, frying pans, socks, food ... but you don't sell memories. I think making memories takes a bit of courage for people who easily write cheques, but can't write out feelings.

What have you got to lose? You're losing a chance to put deposits into your spouse's and children's emotional bank account. At school, each child is required to give a Valentine to every member of the class so no one is left out or feels rejected. Why take your family for granted? Perhaps a valentine's letter is the springboard for enriching your marriage.

Try a caring list. The "Caring List" exercise comes from Lonnie Barbach's *Loving Together Workbook*. Make a list of at least 10 things that your partner does, or could do, for you that make you feel cared for; then add to the list each day. These could be small things like calling from work (including the tractor or the barn), kissing you goodbye, planning a night on the town, or complimenting you on how you look. All the items on the list should be what you want your partner to start to do, or continue to do. Once you each have a caring list, carry out three items on your partner's list each day! Make loving memories today and leave your family a legacy that can't be bought!

MATCHMAKER: HIRING A LOVE CONSULTANT
JANUARY 1998

"A farmstead without a woman about is a bleak place."
– farmer Alf Bryan

Perhaps you're a male farmer, 40, secure, "seeking a potential life mate with good values and the right attitude to share the good life." Maybe you fit the older widow, SWF (single white female) category: "caring, honest, ethical; likes gardening, canning, cooking and other farm work. Looking to share life and laughter."

Seeking that special someone is a tough road in rural areas. How does a single farmer or young professional woman find a life partner on the prairies? The mail-order bride books are in the museums. In the '90s you can use a dating service, hire a matchmaker, or advertise in the personal columns in the papers or on the Internet.

What's the difference in these approaches? A dating service lets the members choose their match, whereas matchmaker does the choosing for members. After talking to three professional matchmakers, I would consider them to be "Love Coaches."

After each match, a good matchmaker gets feedback from both parties about compatibility and suitability. She develops a good feel for individual preferences and personalities.

After careful study of all types of services, Connections (a Dallas-based company) chose matchmaking because their market research showed it is successful for the greatest number of people.

Why would you join a matchmaking service? Personally, the bar scene is not the way I'd want to meet people. As a busy farmer, you've thrown your heart into your business, and now need a safe, more focused way to meet people. If you're shy, and prefer meeting one-on-one, instead of large crowds, matchmaking is worth a try.

How do you find a matchmaker? Diane Mowbray, a farm wife from Roland, Manitoba, runs Candlelight International Matchmakers. She sends clients a detailed application form, and arranges an interview. Mowbray meets women in their homes, and men at restaurants. The in-depth personal interview helps Mowbray assess each situation. "How to overcome the initial hesitation of meeting someone new is hard work, " Mowbray confides. "Clients see themselves as starting over like a teenager, even in their forties or sixties." After the interview, Mowbray checks two references very discreetly, and makes a match.

One gentleman was coaxed by Mowbray's gentle manner to phone a lady. He said that he would "give it a try." They talked on the phone for two hours! He reported back to Mowbray promptly, and the couple will be meeting face-to-face soon.

Lianne Tregobov of Camelot Introductions in Winnipeg, has been matchmaking for five years. She stresses that finding the right match is "not necessarily a fast process" to a long-term relationship. Tregobov suggests consumers work with "credible, experienced companies" and shop around to get answers.

How do I meet someone who understands farming and country life? You choose a matchmaker that has rural clientele. Candlelight, Camelot, and Country Introductions are places to start. Cindy Blenkarn met her husband via a personal service, and she made matches from Tofield, Alberta with 90 per cent rural clientele as "Country Introductions." Blenkarn uses a database, interviews, and members' choices from their age pool. She says the majority of her clients are 35 to 55, and the bar scene is "dying off." Ladies are usually willing to relocate. Her latest success story is a gentleman with two teenagers who is marrying a woman with two teens; everyone likes the match!

If you're single, looking for someone special and are "tired of meeting the wrong people," maybe it is time to hire a love coach.

The right matchmaker can help you find someone who is a good fit for you. All people registered with matchmakers are pre-screened. They don't accept all applicants, and they ask about criminal history.

What will it cost? Fees in 1998 ranged from $150 to $321. Fees are sometimes negotiable. The fees entitle you, for example, to five introductions, being introduced to one person at a time.

Mowbray considers a relationship that is ongoing for six months or more to be match.

Tregobov's firm celebrated 20 marriages in 1997. Blenkarn was busy with 11 interviews in 10 days, just prior to Christmas.

A good matchmaker gives you feedback, and individualized ongoing attention. Based on her assessments and your criteria, she connects you to people that will value your time, and your tender heart. Don't be scared to get married because you're afraid you might lose the farm. Invest in the professional services of a matchmaker and let the "love coach" bring a soul mate to your family and farm. "Farmers find themselves getting the farm established as the first priority, and then they think about a wife later," adds Mowbray.

It takes two to make a match. Matchmakers also encourage women of all ages to overcome their hesitancy and arrange for an interview for the opportunity to enjoy country life with their new mate. The challenge of meeting someone who is a potential life partner can be met using professional help. Matchmaking is a very serious business, with many happy outcomes. Godspeed to you single men and women seeking a mate for your journey.

FIVE EASY WAYS TO SAY "I LOVE YOU"
FEBRUARY 2001

You wouldn't dare think of leaving the farmyard with the Chevy truck tank showing "empty" but have you checked your wife's tank lately? Each of us has a "love tank," the feeling that we are appreciated and loved by our family. Sometimes over long stretches in the busyness of family life we forget to check if our loved ones are "running on empty." If you are frustrated waiting for the next cheque, and feeling like your emotional bank account is in the red, here's some fuel for your home's love fire:

- **Words of affirmation.** "I'm really glad I married you. You are my best friend. I appreciate how you listen to me. Thank you for loving me." When we speak word of encouragement to our mates it is like giving them a gift. Using kind tones, taking the time to listen, and making eye contact really help us connect. A beautiful card or a care-fully written letter tucked under the pillow is a great place to start. Words are powerful, high-octane fuel for love!

- **Togetherness.** Okay, it's calving season, and you haven't been off the farm together for a hotel get-away for 10 years. You really like being together, but are you having fun doing activities you both enjoy? If you feel loved just by spending quality time with your spouse, plan something special. For us, it is a moonlit walk down the lane, or a ski across the quarter to see how much snow is on the field. Find activities that help you focus on each other for moments of quality of time.

- **Doing things for your spouse.** What things can I do for my mate that makes him or her feel cared for? Maybe you'll clean the vehicle, inside and out, that heads to that off-farm job everyday. Be creative. Make a list of the ways you like to be cared for, and pay attention. "Making warm meals" heads my hubby's list.

- **Show affection in meaningful ways.** This is the fastest way to fill my love tank. I grew up in a family of huggers and kissers. I ask for hugs and kisses when I'm washing dishes, and need lots of physical touch to feel loved. Our kids like this way of showing love the best; they told me so. If your spouse feels hurt when the hugs don't come, maybe you can talk about ways to have more touch in your relationship. Ask for what you need! Have fun finding out!

- **Roses and wrenches.** Flowers are a visual symbol of love, and I'll be thrilled with a $5 rose any day! Some people's love tanks are filled when they receive gifts. You may have gifts in the shed waiting to be discovered. Spray paint those antique heavy irons black and present them to your mate as new bookends … refinish a family heirloom. Flashlight batteries and wrenches also signal to your mate that you are thinking of things that make his or her life easier!

To find out more about the ways to show love in your family read *The Five Love Languages* by Gary Chapman. Happy Valentines!

DATE YOUR MATE ON VALENTINE'S DAY
FEBRUARY 1995

The spark needed to rekindle loving memories of your wedding day can be as close as the community hall or church this Valentine's Day. Ten years ago in Boissevain, Manitoba, a creative group of farm women hosted a Valentine's party with a wedding theme.

Imagine the fun of wearing your wedding dress to a special candlelight dinner with your husband, February 14. If the dress no longer fits or zips, bring it along for a wall decoration. Husbands can wear their wedding suit or a tuxedo!

Sharing laughter while reviewing wedding photos of members of the community brings opportunities to get to know each other better. As a "newer" bride in Boissevain in 1985, I really appreciated the family history revealed by wedding albums which span the decades. My connection to other farm brides became stronger.

Couples can stand under a trellis for a Valentine photograph. Brides may wear corsages or carry silk bouquets (it is winter!), and husbands may don a boutonniere. The local video-camera buff could be enlisted to record the wedding date fun.

Chuckles and giggles will fill the room when three couples representing various generations are chosen to candidly answer questions in the "Newlywed Game". One couple won the game at our event by answering the question: "Has your wife ever burned anything?" "No!"

Asking couples to list the various terms of endearments they share is another quiz that's fun. I recall that "Honeybuns" and "Sweet cheeks" were unique to the pair who won the contest. The fact that I can recall such trivia 10 years later is proof of the memories created. Roars of laughter would break out as the master of ceremonies reviewed the master list of endearments until a couple was chosen for using a particularly tender phrase.

Guests who are poetically inclined may produce some romantic prose to enhance the mood of the evening. A short slide-show (or PowerPoint) of honeymoon adventures may also be enlightening!

Decorative touches of cinnamon hearts, bright tapered candles, flowers, place cards, red cloth napkins and table linens create a festive atmosphere of romance.

Those who are single, or no longer married, may enjoy the evening, too. They may be guests, or be happy to help serve the dinner. Couples who don't wish to bake their cake and eat it too, may prefer to use local caterers. If a potluck supper or dessert smorgasbord is your choice, your group will be able to reduce costs by providing the food for the Valentine's party.

Cupid's gift: Nurturing the love and commitment in our marriages should be an ongoing process. "Though the passion may wane, the fire doesn't have to die," as my sister says. Cupid's gift to your Valentine may be a party, or simply a piece of paper. My friend's most precious gift from her farming husband was a collection of 12 paper promises to have a special date every month of the year.

Celebrating their marriage all over again with wedding memorabilia may draw couples closer. The fun can be as close as your local hall, church or someone's home. And you may have a second honeymoon, too!

Looking for Love in all the Right Places
November 2004

A few years ago I received a wedding invitation from a grateful reader, who wanted to share his joy as a farmer in finding a life mate. He had been wondering about how to find a wife, and he read my article on matchmakers. It worked.

At a recent seminar in Alberta, we studied a family farm case where the 25-year-old son was single, and his future choice of a life partner would have a great impact on the farm business. This was a "human resources" issue and it was suggested that a single guy is not going to "troll the high school hallways" looking for a spouse and potential partner for the farm.

In July, I met with some young leading-edge farmers who wanted to know more about my matchmaking friend, Diane Mowbray. Diane professionally matches farmers to spouses. One fellow was pleased that he had met someone by getting out more to golf, curl and play baseball. He had made a conscious decision to get out and socialize at least once a week! Being intentional for this young farmer has paid off!

Finding and choosing a mate is a big deal, and not many farmers want to talk that openly about it. My take at the Alberta discussion was to question "how attractive are you?" You'll spend lots of money on researching equipment, or crop inputs, but what time, energy and focus are you spending on making yourself a great person to commit to?

Ponder my list:

- **Shows love and appreciation.** Do you know what your love language is? Do you need verbal affirmation, gifts, time, acts of service, or meaningful touch?

- **Listens and shares.** We all need space to talk, and feel like people are listening to us. Would you consider personal counseling to improve your communication skills? Do you know your core passions and values?

- **Cherishes the specialness of the relationship and celebrates it.** People don't like to be taken for granted. Take time to celebrate special occasions.

- **Balances work and family time, and knows how to have fun.** It doesn't surprise me that my friend found new love when he decided to have some fun with friends and get off the farm! Workaholics are lazy with relationships, and not very attractive!

- **Has strong self-esteem.** People who have strong self awareness and like themselves are attractive to others. Read *Now, Discover Your Strengths* by Clifton and Buckingham to figure out your five strongest personality themes. It's fun! (www.strengthsfinder.com)

- **Collaborates on solving conflict issues with healthy family boundaries.** Most 25- year-olds don't want to be bugged about the fact that they aren't married. The average age of marriage in Manitoba is 30. Can you talk about tough or sensitive issues with good conflict resolution skills? A farm family business team that knows how to handle disagreements is more attractive than a fighting, "toxic" family.

- **Has a business mindset; someone who manages well.** Farming is a roller-coaster of challenges, and you better be prepared to work as team, and stay for the ride – a long ride. How well does your date understand the farm business culture?

- **Is a lifelong learner.** You are willing to grow, transition and change. You understand that the only person you can change is yourself.

- **Has a support system beyond the marriage.** It is a great day when a married person realizes that not all his or her needs can be met by a spouse. We all need supportive connections beyond the couple relationship. How's your faith?

- **Knows that money doesn't buy happiness; and good relationships do bring joy.** You can have extensive business plans and strategies, but it is less meaningful if you struggle with finding committed lifelong relationships.

Finding a life mate can be a challenge if you think that living on a farm is not glamorous. There are lifestyle issues, but finding someone who shares the same heart for agriculture as you do may take some perseverance and determination. Check out www.eharmony.com and take the personality profile. Commit to find ways to be an attractive life mate. Be intentional. I'm looking forward to receiving more wedding invitations!

PONDER AND PLANT:

What seeds of love do you need to sow? How full is your family's love tank? _____

_____

_____

_____

_____

_____

_____

_____

_____

_____

CHAPTER 9

SPRING AND EASTER

PLANTING THE SEED OF HOPE
APRIL 1995 (MY FIRST COLUMN)

*"Love is patient, love is kind. It is not rude, it is not
self-seeking, it is not easily angered, it keeps no record of
wrongs. It always protects, always trusts, always hopes, always
perseveres. Love never fails."* – 1 Corinthians 13:4-8

Planting barley seed on Palm Sunday is a spring tradition at
our house. Green barley sprouts burst forth to nestle
coloured eggs, symbolizing new life as we celebrate Easter's
message of hope.

I love spring on the farm, the anticipation of a new crop year,
with fervent hope that the combination of proper cultivation,
and waiting on the heavens will produce a bumper harvest.

Some of my friends are not hopeful for spring. They see it as
a time to endure long stretches of tension. A sense of abandon-
ment from their spouses pervades their thinking. They fear signs
of emotional problems like insomnia, anxiety, and excessive
moodiness.

Spring seeding tensions can become an opportunity to assess
our emotional well being and make some changes. Dr. William
C. Menninger's "Seven Criteria for Emotional Maturity" offers
steps for living better emotionally:

1. **Face reality.** If we are healthy, we have, through necessity, learned how to accept frustration with a fair degree of grace. Farm families need to exercise much grace and patience while waiting for warm soil or tractor repairs! Being able to deal constructively with the realities of seeding-time setbacks means we've gleaned those character traits that help us persevere with a positive attitude during tough times.

2. **Adapt to change.** I've often repeated that "change is inevitable, growth is optional." A life-threatening illness, an accident, or a family member's depression are all things our family has had to deal with during spring seeding. Someone once said, "When you realize life is hard, it gets so much easier." People who are depressed need treatment and your support; they need to hear your message of hope and friendship.

3. **Control anxieties.** Level with yourself. Be honest with who you are. Understand that people use escape-like defence mechanisms. After a long day in the field, a farmer may rationalize staring at the TV rather than spending time with the family. Blaming others for your own faults or problems is another defence mechanism that can lead to unjustified conflict.

4. **Give of yourself.** The world could use a lot more givers with a servant attitude. What is your passion or vision? To plant straight rows or nurture healthy, giving children? Keep your passions alive for emotional well being.

5. **Consider others.** Check some of the personality traits affecting your capacity to relate with hope to others. Are you sincere? Evaluate your integrity, honesty, fairness, dependability and ability to accept criticism. Check out the source. If there is truth to the criticism, make some adjustments. If the criticism is unfounded, move ahead.

6. **Curb hostility.** Steel-toed boots have probably saved a few feet when tires are kicked in frustration. Direct hostile ener-

gy into and constructive outlets – like golf! Guilt and unreasonable feelings of inferiority are signs of hostility turned inward. We are hostile when we are unkind, inconsiderate or thoughtless. Meals to the field during seeding could be delivered with warmth, grace and humour. Don't be hostile if you aren't thanked for the task or the meal is set aside.

7. **Learn to care.** The most important yardstick for living better emotionally is the capacity to love – that is, caring. Planting a good crop takes planning, patience, perseverance, passion, and the blessings of providence. These ingredients will also help the seed of hope flourish in your family.

BRINGING OTHERS HOPE
APRIL 2000

"I am the resurrection and the life. He who believes in me will live, even though he dies; and whoever lives and believes in me will never die." – John 11:25, 26 (NIV)

Soon it will be time for my favorite celebration of the year – Easter! I look forward to hearing the stories of Jesus. Children waving palm branches to welcome Him to Jerusalem. Feasting with the men who gave up their fishing nets to follow Him. Praying alone. Trying to fathom the pain and suffering of dying by hanging from a cross. Rejoicing that Easter morning brings hope. Jesus was not in the tomb. He rose from the dead. He conquered death. He gives us the hope of eternal life with Him.

Are you looking for hope? Marilyn Adams, founder of Farm Safety 4 Just Kids writes:

> *"Hope is a gift given to you by others.*
> *It is wrapped within the embrace of a friend*
> *or the words of a stranger.*
> *Hope is also a gift you give to yourself. But only*
> *when the time is right.*

When, finally, you are ready to begin to heal.
Like anyone who experiences profound loss,
this was unknown to me at first."

Adam's book, *Rhythm of the Seasons,* shares her story of how the tragic loss of her son in a farm accident changed her life. Friends and strangers came bearing the gift of hope, and healing took place.

That sense of hope, knowing that there is more to life than just the things we experience here on earth, is why Easter is my favourite celebration. I am encouraged, comforted, elated, and thankful that when I die, that is not the end.

Hope is an expectation and a desire combined. Christians who believe in the hope of eternal life desire to give that gift to family, friends, even strangers. Bringing others hope is basically what Easter all about. Desperate, broken, hurting people can find forgiveness and unconditional acceptance from a loving God. God sent His Son Jesus to give us the promise of eternal life, the hope of heaven.

Share the good news of Easter with your family and neighbours. Answer the children's questions about the true meaning behind the festive celebrations of Easter Sunday. Before the rush of spring seeding begins, pause to count the many blessings in your life now and forever, because the life of Jesus brings you hope.

WHY EASTER GIVES ME HOPE
APRIL 2001

New life, great joy, the hope of resurrection, are all great encouragement to families who know the true meaning of Easter. I plant barley seed about 10 days before Easter Sunday to have a thick green grassy display for the Easter eggs to nest in, while outdoors it may still be mucky and dull.

Many farm families are feeling bogged down and dull on the inside this spring. I received an e-mail from Dr. Val Farmer, a

Fargo-based psychologist, who also counsels farm families. I've been reading Dr. Farmer's book, *Honey, I Shrunk the Farm, a Rural Stress Survival Guide.* Dr. Farmer had hoped another collection of farm survival strategies would be behind him in the '80s, but here we are again.

"I was just in Estevan, Saskatchewan and felt first-hand the discouragement among Canadian farmers there. For the first time in many years farmers are trying to sell or rent land with no takers. Many farmers don't have farming heirs, they look ahead at the direction of agriculture and would like to get out of farming but feel trapped in the present circumstances. I don't think I've seen this situation where there is land available and no optimistic farmer willing to expand. It is a sad commentary of how bad things are," writes Dr. Farmer.

Who feels like celebrating Easter when circumstances are so dark? Easter is the resurrection of Jesus Christ from the dead, breaking through darkness forever! He is risen, He is risen indeed! Christians, followers of Jesus, have the hope of eternal life because they are in a close relationship with the One who died for them. This hope of heaven and the assurance that God is with them in all things is like a solid rock foundation for all avenues of the believer's life.

Why do I have hope at Easter? I believe that Jesus cares for me, and wants me to experience the joy of eternal life, now, in 2001, with the expectation that when I die, I will go to the place He has ready for me. Farm families can support each other by offering the hope that God cares about their every need, and all their pain.

Our Sunday School class is studying the series on Mental Health and the Church entitled "No Longer Alone" by Dr. James Toews. Mental illness strikes some people, but all of us have to deal with mental health issues when our temperaments and personalities are angry, sad, frustrated and just not coping in healthy ways. The whole point of "No Longer Alone" is to develop empathy for those who are hurting, walk alongside, listen, and listen some more. We don't have to have all the answers, but we are called to be in relationship with others.

I can't fathom the pain and anger you are experiencing as you contemplate not planting anything this spring. I do know that God cares about you. My hope is that people who have a vital, intimate relationship with God will reach out to listen to your struggles and encourage you.

Our church banner is a bright white Easter lily with the cross rising from the core of the flower. On Good Friday, the day we remember Christ's ultimate sacrifice for our sins by dying on the cross, the banner is silent. On Easter Sunday the words "He is Risen" appear to herald the greatest hope of all for those despairing or fearing death.

I'd encourage you to go to church this Easter Sunday, to soak in God's love, warmth and hope. Crack open your Bible, sit in a ray of sunshine, and read the entire Gospel of John.

There is a time for everything, and a season for every activity under heaven. I pray that this Easter, you will find an anchor of hope for your farm family.

YOUR DEEPEST NEEDS
APRIL 2004

"If you hold on to my teaching, you are really my disciples. Then you will know the truth, and the truth will set you free."
– John 8:31, 32

I asked my Sunday School class, a faithful group of farmers and rural folks, "How do you find out what someone really needs?" They shared their thoughts on listening deeply, spending time with people to build relationships, and relying on God to give wisdom. We've learned how we are all shaped differently by our experiences in life, and yet every person can show love by connecting with someone and pointing the way to a relationship with God.

At Easter I am excited to share in the celebration of the resurrection of Jesus Christ, the Son of God. This year I have images in my mind that are new. I attended the film "The Passion." The small brown pamphlet I found at the back of the theatre is something that none of the film's critics will discuss. It offers answers to your deepest needs:

- pure love,
- everlasting life,
- complete forgiveness,
- ultimate wholeness.

"Our greatest felt needs are to be loved, forgiven, whole and alive," writes Brian Mavis. A relationship with Jesus will meet your deepest needs. Readers tell me that they appreciate the times I use scripture, and share the good news of the Gospel. I have written many things this winter about the struggles farm families are facing, yet what sustains those who have faith? I believe that the resurrected life of Jesus gives us "a reason to hope and not just cope." My friends who are coping with a serious illness were encouraged when their doctor said, "You will make it, you are people of faith."

Today, I received a phone call from a frustrated farmer who wonders if he will ever be happy. His needs are to be loved, forgiven, and feel whole and alive. As a Christian I have the greatest treasure, the knowledge that God loves me unconditionally, and that when I die, I will have eternal life in heaven. My sins are forgiven, and my purpose in life is to serve God and tell others about His love for them.

If this is the first Easter that you are truly curious about who Jesus is, I encourage you to read a recent translation of the Bible, and start with the book of John. I like the "Message" translation as it uses today's language. I also encourage you to find a small group to study your questions about Christ, and be connected to Christian people who also struggle, yet know God's goodness in their lives. Call the pastor of your local church and find out how to get connected.

I've done a lot of speaking over the years about living an intentional life, or finding balance in a complex world. Some people think "balance" should be replaced by the word "integration." Whatever you call it, people need to have a sense

> *"Peace, I leave with you; my peace I give you. I do not give to you as the world gives. Do not let your hearts be troubled and do not be afraid."* – John 14:27 (NIV)

of wholeness. My pamphlet from "The Passion" talks about the followers of Jesus being devoted to Him because He took the broken pieces of their lives and gave them the peace of His life.

When I was 15, Jesus met my deepest needs and I committed my life to a relationship with Him. May you find your deepest needs met this Easter, as you accept the gift of eternal life from a loving God who conquered death, and gives us hope. He is risen indeed!

PONDER AND PLANT:

Where are you in your search for hope that lasts?_____

_____

_____

_____

_____

_____

_____

_____

_____

_____

CHAPTER 10

MOM

SPLASHES OF JOY FOR MOM
MAY 2002

"A joyful heart is good medicine, but a broken spirit dries up the bones." – Proverbs 17:22

I was moved by a story of a church group visiting a maximum security prison with stacks of Mother's Day cards. Those sentenced to be away from their moms stood patiently in line to choose a special greeting of love to send to the most important person in their lives. I invite you to choose a verse from this column to enclose in your mom's card this year. Do it while you still have a mom.

For those of you who find it hard to write your feelings on paper, start with this: "I love you Mom. You are special and dear to me. Thanks for all you have done for me over the years." When we realize the power of words, we will take the time to share them.

"Pleasant words are a honeycomb, sweet to the soul and healing to the bones." – Proverbs 16:24

Written affirmation is one of my love languages – one of the ways I feel loved. You might like to ask your children what makes them feel loved. Ask your mother what makes her feel loved. We recently celebrated my mother-in-law's 80th birthday. She sat at a full table of 20 family members and said, "This is the best gift ever to have everyone here. This is what I really wanted." For her, the act of taking the time to celebrate with her made her feel very special.

"For he will give his angels charge concerning you, to guard you in all your ways." – Psalm 91:11

Moms say a lot of prayers for the safety of their children. On farms, keeping the wee ones away from danger is a full-time job. Then the teens cruise late at night, and dads sometimes do double shifts in the field. Moms deliver fuel for the body and machines (and operate the equipment, too!). We take our health for granted until it weakens. Thank your mom this year for her prayers and helping qualities that have enabled you to get where you are today.

"Do not neglect to show hospitality to strangers, for by this some have entertained angels without knowing it." – Hebrews 13:2

Feeling free to invite whoever happens to need feeding to my table is a gift that I learned from my mom. Whatever was on the table was offered to salespeople, truckers, or anyone needing food for body and soul. If you are newly widowed this year, you understand the joy of sharing a meal with another person. Don't spend a lot of time fussing over gourmet recipes, just get the family together around the table for a great time sharing food and good memories. Order in Chinese, chicken, or cheese pizza! It is now considered "special" for families to eat together.

"Do not merely look out for your own personal interest, but also for the interests of others." – Philippians 2:4

"Mom, do you know where my wallet is?" Homemakers tend to have "mommy eyes" and are supposed to know where everyone else's stuff is at all times. As you reflect on how your mom made sacrifices for your benefit, be grateful. If you are an aging parent (actually, we all are aging) you might want to write down a legacy list to pass on to your family. Mention the acts of love you remember. Love is shared in many different ways. Acts of love are a great inheritance.

"Like a shepherd he will tend his flock, in his arm he will gather lambs, and carry them in his bosom; he will gently lead the nursing ewes." – Isaiah 40:11

On my foyer wall hangs a framed card, the picture of a young shepherd girl cradling a lamb in her arms. I love the shepherd images in the Bible, because I identify that Jesus is my Good Shepherd. I feel loved unconditionally by God. I was deeply loved and hugged by my mother. I am blessed. Thank your mom for her meaningful touch in your life. If she didn't hug you a lot, maybe she showed you love with her eyes, or in her acts of serving you.

"For where your treasure is, there will your heart be also."
– Matthew 6:21

I believe relationships are the greatest treasures. My relationship to a living and loving God gives me the hope of heaven. Relationships to family are a priority in how I spend my time. Connecting to community is also nurtured in very intentional ways. Share these verses with your mom in a carefully written card. She deserves a splash of joy this year.

THANKS FOR LIFE!
MAY 1998

I'm a mom. I need to be appreciated. When I heard my son say "Thank you for my wonderful parents" when he was talking to God I was thankful, too. Our son also prayed "Thank you that I was born." His birthmother gave him the gift of life. He doesn't know what abortion is, but he knows that a young woman chose to bring him into the world.

Mother's Day is full of lovely cards, flowers and hugs, but for some it is a painful reminder of loss of a child, or a relationship. I'd encourage you to embrace life and choose to support moms – all shapes, ages, and situations. Manitoba has the highest teenage pregnancy rate in Canada; lots of young moms needing nurturing before and after the birth. Again, the issue of how precious life is stares us in the face as decisions for health care and emotional and physical well-being are made.

I had always hoped to have four children, but am thankful for two. I am sensitive to those yearning women and men who would love to have children, but can't. Adoption would be such a positive option, but many unborn babies are killed in our country. Birthmothers who release their child to another family need love and understanding in practical ways. Many of today's "open adoptions" afford ongoing communication with birthparents and the adoptive families.

Our son requested a special birthday gift for his twelfth birthday, he wanted to meet his birthmother. We have an "open" adoption relationship, whereby yearly written contact with our son's birthparents has kept all the families in touch since our son was born. His birthmother was thrilled to meet him, give hugs, and marvel at the joy of re-uniting.

As adoptive parents we prepared for the reunion with the following thoughts:

"It's okay to search and connect with your birth family. You do love your adoptive family even when you want to relate to your birth family. Knowing your birth family will help complete the circle and fill in the missing pieces for you, the adoptee. It won't weaken our relationship as adoptive parents. Talking about our true feelings about adoption will cause better understanding and good emotional health. Asking questions about your birthparents is important and not a sign of disrespect to your adoptive parents. Birthmothers think about their babies every day. They love them dearly. Birthparents are people who hurt and seek healing, too."

Why consider an adoption reunion? Michelle McColm, author of *Adoption Reunions* says:

- You can learn about your birth family and explore feelings.
- A reunion can compensate for the feelings of being different.
- A meeting can help you feel completely accepted by the birth family.
- Reunions help birthmothers resolve grief.

"Reunions provide healing. With courage, love and compassion, there are long-term gains for everybody," adds McColm, an adoptee. Her book is a goldmine of support and practical advice for all parties – the adoptee, birthparents and adoptive parents. She ends each chapter with a list of things to remember:

- **For those searching:** make sure you're mentally, emotionally, and financially ready and have a support system in place.
- **For all:** It is okay to be focussed, harmful to be too obsessed. Strive for balance.
- **Adoptee:** You know you are adopted, your birthmother's family might not. Search carefully.
- **Birthmother:** Most adoptees are not ready to meet their birthmothers until their mid to late twenties. (Our son got the idea from his adopted cousin who met her birthmother a year earlier. A social worker told us that males usually don't request reunions until their spouses or girlfriends pressure them to do so!)
- **Adoptive parents:** A search doesn't mean you've failed as parents.

McColm suggests that pre-reunion counselling is a good idea, and finding a support group like Parent Finders. "As adoptees and birth families meet, healing can take place... Alongside many other self-help groups...post-adoption support groups help reunitees to complete their emotional and psychological development, and to claim their birthright as fully integrated human beings with a present, a future and a past."

As soon as the word was out that we were part of a reunion, amazing stories came my way. One fellow met his motorcycle-driving birthmother and discovered she also had a passion for tattoos and bikes like he did. He was thankful for the meeting, as she died within the year! My friend has a great relationship with her birthfather, and feels pieces of her life now fit together better. Our son knows he is deeply loved by us and his birth family.

Whether you have one mom or two, celebrate the life your mother gave to you! I hope you'll hear the encouraging words: "I love you, Mom. Thanks for giving me the gift of life." Happy Mother's Day.

SEASONS
NOVEMBER 1998

November is a time for remembering. We remember loved ones who never came home from the war or, in my case, family (my mom) who won't be around to celebrate Christmas this year. It's a mixed month for me. It is the 10th anniversary of losing my sister to a collision with a drunk driver; and the celebration of our son's 10th birthday. He was born two weeks after the accident.

These thoughts are not intended to invoke pity, but rather reflection. I invite you to reflect on the changing seasons of life. Don't wait for bad news to appreciate your life; treasure you life right now.

Sitting by a loved one in a palliative care unit, waiting for them to die is a precious experience in treasuring life, and letting go. As I sat basking in the sunbeams of my mom's hospital room in September, I had several hours to reflect on the many gifts of love she bestowed on me for more than 40 years. The nursing assistant who watched me interact with other grieving families on the ward had a gift for me ... the gift of his words. Words are powerful in healing, so it is an honour to share Winnipegger Timothy Lawrence's poem entitled "Seasons":

Were I able to halt the passing of a dear life
I would surely swiftly intervene
Yet I am helpless and frail
A feeble bystander
Respectfully sad and serene
Could I but turn back life's tenacious clock
I would make it my devoted role
But I am mute and weak
A grieving furious witness
To the passing of a soul
If I could wish, it would be for eternal summer
I'd cherish the warmth so pleasing
Fond memories most treasured
Glowing nostalgia reminds
Of that most perfect season
Tis the season of love and growth
Fences strong' neath the long summer sun
Children at play
Laughter rings strong
The essence of life in everyone
Might I be brave, might I be forgiving
And forgiven when Autumn comes my way
Preparing for God's feast
Midst loved ones and family
Night surrenders to an endless joyful day
This is the season of our frailty
When flesh and spirit deem to part
Burdens uplifting
Rewards unfolding
Not an end but a glorious start
Had I the means to melt away the winter
It would truly not be done for myself

Grief must be sustained
Till endured and conquered
Then put away upon memory's shelf
This is the season of shared restful hope
To be consoled and to provide consolation
Carrying the torch
Fulfilling dreams
Binding the ties of each generation
If I could describe the rapture of Spring
Like melting snow are pain and strife
I am reborn
The undying spirit of love
provides a new and perfect life
This is the season of resurrection and glory
Spring rains upon seeds newly planted
Mysteries revealed
Fears reconciled
God's promise of ecstasy granted
If I were to bestow a single message from my heart
To the grieving or those soon to grieve
Notice the seasons
Their meaning
Is a beautiful reason to believe
These are the Seasons of God's blessed plan
And from them we find a pathway
Winter passes
Spring will emerge as surely as night beckons day

CHAPTER 11

DAD

COMMUNICATE THE BIG FOUR!
JULY 2002

"Who, being loved, is poor?" – Oscar Wilde

As the mom of a teenage son I was really thankful that Mike Ross handed me a copy of his book *How to Speak Alien, Invading your Teens' World Without Invading Their Space*. Ross has worked with teens for over a decade, and he edits my son's favourite magazine called *Breakaway* published by Focus on the Family.

Ross believes that focused attention from Dad is an important part of building family relationships. Are you a Dad "missing in action"? Ross has a checklist for success that fathers can use to get connected to their teenagers. I think his list also relates to sons and fathers that work together well into their fifties!

Give them your full attention on a daily basis.

Burying your head in the newspaper or being distracted with TV sports tells your family that you are not interested in connecting with them. If you are doing chores together, or riding out to the field together, don't just talk about the weather. "Tell me how your day is going" is a good opener that deserves more than a grunt in response!

> *"We have one life to live and one chance to live it in the richest way possible."* -Judith Thurman

Spend individual time together.

Father's Day is set aside as a day to honour fathers. Fishing at the local dam, playing catch in the backyard, canoeing at a nearby lake, or golfing a few rounds together builds strong bridges for your relationship. Teens want and need your attention but often just don't know how to ask for it.

Communicate the Big Four: "I love you. I am proud of you. I trust you. I am here for you."

When our daughter turned 18 her dad blessed her by writing "I love you and I am proud of you," in her card. He didn't even read Ross's book !

This winter I spoke with readers who were distressed about the relationships they had with farming fathers who just couldn't trust them to take over the farm management. You may have different values than your dad, and he may see things differently than you do, but we all need to hear the words "I love you" even when we agree to disagree. Don't put off communicating the big four.

One of my readers lost his dad to a heart attack just days after we spoke. I thought of what preacher C.H. Spurgeon says, "Those who loved you and were helped by you will remember you. So carve your name on hearts and not on marble."

We shop around for the best deals on new grain bins, equipment and livestock. How much time do we invest in the human capital on our farms? Father's Day is just one day of 365 that you can make a special effort to show your dad how much you care about your relationship. If you don't have a father, you might want to drop a note of encouragement to that man in your life who has been a role model or mentor.

THE GIFT OF TOUCH
JUNE 1995

"A wise man will hear and increase in learning, and a man of understanding will acquire wise counsel." – Proverbs 1:5

One Father's Day, I put a pile of wax crayon shavings on the front of a blank white paper, and stuck the artwork down with clear vinyl. The handwritten black ink message inside read: "Dear Dad. Thank you for making my life so colourful and giving me your boundless love and big hugs. I am really blessed to have such great memories of a happy childhood. I love you dearly." This card is still pinned to the wall above my father's dresser. I think he liked it!

My dad blessed me with lots of hugs and kisses as a child, a teen and as an adult. I went to bed every night knowing and feeling that I was loved as my parents said "Good night precious." Today, I am always greeted with a big hug and kiss. The gift of touch is meaningful touch.

Researchers describe meaningful touch as a gentle touch, stroke, kiss or hug given by significant people in our lives. "Touch becomes meaningful when the one touching desires to bless the one touched and reaches out for his or her benefit, not one's own," write Gary Smalley and John Trent in *The Blessing Workbook: How to give and receive the approval we all need.*

Today's awareness of the abuse of touch, particularly sexual abuse, cautions us all to give meaningful, appropriate touch. It is a sad scenario that this cloud of negative touch has dimmed some people's desire to touch anyone at all for fear of reprisal. We can still give handshakes, pats on the shoulder, "high-fives," and tousle our kids' or give "bear hugs" to our friends and family.

My dad's willingness to give me lots of affection all my life has given me a deep sense of his acceptance. I counsel farm families to start making affirming connections with their adult children, just with the loving glance of eye contact, or a hand on the shoulder. The touch of a father communicates blessing to the

> *"Somehow, year after year, Dad managed to take us on vacations he couldn't afford to provide, in order to make memories that we couldn't afford to be without."* – Richard Exley

child, and warmth. Mothers know, too, the responses of new-born babies who soak up all the touch they can as they thrive and grow.

Think of the symbolism of two lovers holding hands, shaking hands as a greeting in business, putting your hand on the shoulder of the son who has just wrapped a machine around the hydro pole, or embracing grandpa at the airport. Kids who leave home with a hug before the school bus arrives have started the day off right!

What does the gift of touch do for us? It makes us feel good inside and gives a sense that we are accepted and affirmed with love. The literature abounds with the theme of "therapeutic" touch where it has a positive effect on our health. A study by Dr. Delores Kreiger, at New York University, found that touching caused the body tissues to get more oxygen, and this increase of oxygen energizes a person and can aid in healing.

The biggest impact of meaningful touch is its effect on our ability to develop good relationships. Fathers, I encourage you to keep affirming your daughters; don't stop hugging them when they are 9! I have listened to pleas of young teens for the past 10 years and the frequent request, "I wish my dad would give me a hug."

Neglecting to meaningfully touch our kids starves them of genuine acceptance ... so much so that it can drive them into the arms of someone who is all too willing to touch them.

This month when you meet family and friends at graduation, a wedding, an auction, or the local coffee shop try touching them. Think about how the touch you offer makes you feel in regard to that other person. Small safe acts of touch, can be a quick back rub, a high five, a pat on the shoulder, holding hands as you speak, or gently clasping the other person's hand in your hands.

My friend's grandfather always clasped both his hands around the person who extended one hand to him for a handshake; she is convinced that this gesture gave her grandfather a powerful way of connecting with other people.

What is stopping you from giving the gift of touch? Here are some ideas for overcoming your resistance.

- Hug children. I know seniors who are not "huggers" with their children, but will not say goodbye to the grandkids without a big hug! Amazing – the power of little people.

- Begin with safe touch, make contact, but not so close that you make the other person uneasy.

- Ask for a hug. Love doesn't read minds. When I need a hug from my family I simply ask with open arms.

- Check out your emotional attitude towards the person you have trouble touching.

- Ask yourself, in what way could meaningful touch improve the relationship?

- How and when will you start giving the gift of touch?

- Ask your family and friends for feedback on what particular touch from you meant the most to them.

I write these words of encouragement to you with tears in my eyes. Teens who are graduating into life this month really need to go with the blessing of their parents. You, fathers and mothers, have the power to give the gift of meaningful touch to your children and extended families. Yes, it is hard work, but farm families know all about hard work. Yes, it will take time to heal past hurts, but time is needed to commit yourself to meaningful touch of your loved ones.

FATHER CARE STRATEGIES
JUNE 2004

His eyes glistened as he spoke softly to his son. "I have worked very hard for many years to build this farm. I am thankful to have a son who can manage when I'm gone. It makes me feel good to keep this farm in our family name. I am willing to continue to do whatever it takes to keep things going. I'm doing this for you."

"I appreciate everything you stand for Dad. I am thankful for your strong work ethic that you have modeled for me. I am grateful for you sharing your assets with me, to help me get started. I am not being disrespectful when I disagree with you, it is just that some ways of doing things have changed."

Fathers and sons create a strong dynamic business team when they can communicate clearly with each other, and work through conflict issues as a business management strategy.

Life on the farm can be hectic and stressful when the farm team takes each other for granted. Here's the question I want you to answer: What are your father care strategies?

I am blessed with a farming dad who has always been affectionate, hard-working, gentle, and generous to others. I have witnessed his tears of joy when I married, tears of grief when he buried my mom, and tears of hurt when family issues stung.

As a farm family coach, it has been my privilege to sit in a very sacred space with families sharing business discussions that drew out deep emotion and feeling. I would ask the father to speak about his expectations for his future, and look his son in the eye as he spoke. I would nudge the son to listen deeply, and then reflect back his appreciation and expectation of the life on the farm he hoped to create.

My life lesson from my coaching is: take time to show your dad how much you care about him. I would suggest that words are a very powerful gift. Making the time to write your father a letter of gratitude is the most priceless gift you can bestow on a man who has battled a tough farming year.

Marty Seligman's *Authentic Happiness* course (www.authentichappinesscoaching.com) encourages his students to write a gratitude letter which they must hand deliver to a person who needs to know how important they are. It forces the writer to slow down and realize what you have to be thankful for. It can also be powerful in restoring or starting the healing of a broken relationship.

The great thing about a letter is that it can be read over and over again. I have a file called "My silver box file" where I keep notes of encouragement that I receive. Imagine your dad's delight as he re-reads your letter placed above his dresser, or pinned on his office bulletin board for encouragement to keep on going strong.

I often hear: "But you have no idea how hard it is for me to put my thoughts on paper, especially about my father!" Precisely, that's the point. Talk about his special qualities, precious memories growing up and how deeply your dad has affected your life. Your letter of gratitude will be like a shot of adrenalin that gives new energy to continue on. Words carefully crafted will be more valuable than the net worth statement. Parents dream about leaving a legacy to their children, and your letter is a part of helping your father know the gifts he's given are a wonderful blessing to you!

For those of you who "can't write" or "don't have time," make an effort and bust all the excuses. Your father wants respect, relationship and your reflection of gratitude. Today is all you've got. There are no guarantees that you will outlive your dad, and procrastination is poison. I have witnessed huge relief when appreciation is shared openly with parents by their children. Words have a lasting quality when they are committed to paper. Make it your father care strategy this June to tell your dad what he means to you. It might mean the difference between going on or giving up.

BUILDING THE FATHER-DAUGHTER BOND
JUNE 2001

Happy Father's Day! Fathers play a critical role in nurturing their children. The bond between a father and daughter can shape a woman's future relationships with men, and her career aspirations. I recently met a woman who has moved home to care for her aging dad. This woman said: "Dad and I didn't like each other much when I was young, in fact he gave me my first compliment when I was 21! We've worked a lot of things out now, and it is a good thing because Dad may die soon!"

Supportive dads raise daughters who reach a higher level of achievement and choose good mates. The relationship between father and daughter is two-fold:

1) Dad is a parent.
2) Father is a model for all men! He encourages respect by showing it to the daughter. "When a father respects his daughter, she is more likely to feel competent and capable," notes Carole Isenberg, a relationship mentor.

What do you need to teach your daughter?

- Teach her that Mom and Dad are equals. Take a look at the way you treat women, as well as your relationship with her mother. Even if you are supportive of your daughter, you can be saying you disrespect women when you tell sexist jokes or belittle your wife.

- Teach her to solve problems and to deal with conflict and work through anger. Let your daughter struggle as she grows. You can assist in finding answers using encouragement to build self-esteem. Be supportive especially when careless things happen; be available at all times to build trust. I promised my dad not to talk on the cell phone on icy roads moments after we hit the ditch!

- Teach her that perfection is a myth. Encourage risk-taking. It is okay to make mistakes, and learn from them! Challenge physical limits as she helps you with the fencing, sort livestock, moves augers, or other new experiences which are good for growth. Don't simply accept "I'm scared."

- Teach her to ask for what she wants. We live in a culture of changing roles. You can show your approval for non-traditional role models like women running for municipal office.

- BE THERE! Spend uninterrupted time together, listen to each other and encourage new interests. Teach your daughter to fix things, check the oil in her car or manage her finances.

- Compliment your daughter for who she is as a person. Make regular deposits into her emotional bank account . Express your affection freely. Never tease her about her body. Don't be withdrawn; your daughter needs to know you approve of her.

Why bother working at the relationship?

Girls who have close, positive relationships with their fathers tend to have positive self-identity, good mental health, and a healthy attitude toward men. You may find the nurturing and loving relationship established in the early years of your farm family pays huge dividends when the farm is transferred. In 95 per cent of cases, the sons will continue the family farm operation. Hopefully, the emotional bank account you have built with your daughter is healthy as she makes good life choices and respects the men she meets in her career. It is never too late to build a strong father-daughter bond.

PONDER AND PLANT:

How can you cultivate a deeper bond with your dad and children?

_____

_____

_____

_____

What's holding you back? _____

_____

_____

_____

_____

CHAPTER 12

GRANDPARENTS

BLESSING GRANDCHILDREN
SEPTEMBER 2002

When our son got his compound bow he couldn't wait to show his grandfather how he could shoot the target; and he let Grandpa try his strength out on the bow, too! These little things mean a lot in the lives of children who may not see grandparents often, or suffer the shuffle of being in a blended family. When you keep your grandkids foremost in your mind they feel valued by you. That's what a blessing is...finding ways to connect to your children's children.

How can you connect with your grandchildren? "Pay attention to the names of their friends, favourite books, sports heroes and music bands," says Deb Gebeke of the North Dakota Extension Service. When you key into what kids are learning and their interests, you'll have a lot of interesting stories to share. Volunteer pieces of your life with a story can also make a connection.

Frame your interactions with the thought "I was thinking of you," and "I want to know how you are doing." Phone calls just to talk to the children or a special e-mail show the child that "You are on their side." One grandmother felt it was worth it to get a toll-free number to encourage her grandchildren to call anytime. And a letter in the mail is still a treat to all ages. You might make it special by using a red envelope, audiotaping a bedtime story, or sending cartoons to your grandchild.

What about divorce? Avoid taking sides. Remaining neutral will help build and maintain relationships with all parties. However, this may be difficult as some adults purposely keep their children away from grandparents. If you are part of this heart-breaking scenario you may bless your grandkids with your loving prayers, and look for ways to bridge the communication gap.

In all new family situations, children need your love and emotional support.

Choose a positive attitude and be patient. Step-family relationships are particularly complex. Interfering with a critical approach is a recipe for disaster. No parents appreciate unsolicited advice. We all tend to be sensitive to well-meaning advice, so be an encourager and gentle listener. It will help the whole family if you can talk to your adult child about your feelings in a non-aggressive way.

If you become an "instant" grandparent to new step-grandchildren, begin spending short periods of time together. Allow the relationships to build gradually. Every person is a unique individual who needs to be loved and accepted just the way they are. Try not to show favouritism, and give kids your time. Buying expensive gifts is not the answer.

Here are a few blessing gifts for grandkids:

- **Time.** Spend one-on-one time with each grandchild. This might mean a special weekend at your house, or a walk, or a game together during family gatherings.

- **Listen.** Do you know the concerns and joys of your grandchild? Building a relationship involves listening to the story of where their life is at. This foundation of unconditional love and attention maybe the bridge of trust for big decision discussions in the future. Your listening and wisdom is a priceless gift.

- **Work together.** Working in the shop, in the kitchen, or in the garden are great times to share companionship with your grandkids.

- **Laugh!** Be a role model to show grandchildren that older people can have fun! At our house we play "Chicken Foot" or Crokinole with the grandparents for lots of laughs and good memories. Growing old can still hold good times!

- **Be a storyteller.** Sharing your history and family traditions gives kids a very strong sense of security and stability. You might want to make family scrapbooks together or just enjoy flipping through photo albums. When you share photos, always be sure to label and date them with a photo-safe wax pencil on the back.

- **"I love you no matter what."** This is the message many need to hear. As a grandparent you are somewhat removed from parenting hassles, and can offer lots of encouragement with "this too shall pass." Problems and behaviour will change, and you still see the child as special, worthy of your love.

- **Adopt a grandchild.** Divorce or death can really divide families. If you are longing for a close relationship with grandkids think about adopting a family of someone close to you. A special "aunt" who fills the shoes of their grandma who died has blessed our children.

Being a blessing to grandchildren is an awesome legacy. Be intentional about the love, time and care you give your family. Count your blessings and be one!

SAYING GOODBYE
MARCH 2000

Two friends have each buried a parent this past week. Funerals are important; they are a celebration of a life special to us and the place to grieve a loss. As I sat planning my mother's funeral a few years ago I was struck by the words on the wall:

The Funeral:

Helps confirm the reality of death.

Provides a climate for mourning and the expression of grief.

Allows the sorrows of one to become the sorrows of many.

Is one of the few times love is given and not expected in return.

Is a vehicle for the community to pay its respects.

Encourages the affirmation of religious faith.

Is a celebration of a life that has been lived as well as a sociological statement that a death has occurred.

(Author unknown, Thomson Chapels)

Funerals help bring a sense of closure. A distraught woman shared with me that she wished her mom would have "let the family" have a funeral because she didn't feel closure.

"Dying is our most personal and irreversible act. We want our loved ones to be treated and remembered in ways that express and show respect for our uniqueness and the special-ness of our relationship with the deceased," Chris Tina Leimer writes in *The Tombstone Traveller's Guide*.

Here are some of my personal experiences with funerals:

- Wheat placed in the casket bouquet and on the luncheon tables provided a symbol of Christian faith. The seeds of faith are sown in the human personality and grow in the mature faith of the Christian. The sown seed must lose its life in order that it may develop and grow and multiply. Death is not the end but the beginning of life eternal. The mature grain in the sheaf is the direct symbol of the Resurrection – the life beyond the grave, the fulfillment of the promise of Jesus Christ. My mom died during harvest; I went to her fields to gather flax and wheat to tie with ribbons for centerpieces. The florist also used wheat to deco-rate the candelabras at the altar and for the casket bouquet.

- A picture on a big screen TV, a still video of a special man, gave the congregation a loving focus at the front of the church. Photo displays in the foyer are very comforting. One creative family member did a collage of pictures for the "service folder" depicting the love of a father in many stages of life.

- Shoes, Bibles, glasses and violas – are all examples of personal effects that with a brief printed description can tell us what was important in the person's life. I always enjoy learning new things about someone, even after they've died.

- Tributes spoken as letters, poems, or a collection of memories are all wonderful informal ways to let the windows of a person's life be opened by various friends and family. A young man sent a tribute to his grandpa who was terminally ill. The grandfather was blessed to receive the letter before his death, and mourners were blessed again to hear the love conveyed by well-timed words as the grandson read his letter. Mail the letter to the living today!

- Balloons at the altar or at the graveside may also have great meaning to children. We used white helium balloons at the chapel's altar to bring a sense of celebration to my mom's funeral. The grandkids released the balloons to the heavens after the graveside ceremony, saying "I love you Grandma."

- Golf balls thrown into the grave of a grandfather who loved to golf – a unique way to say goodbye. I have also seen messages written on a casket with black felt markers, which may cause a few stirs, but it really helped our cousins leave special thoughts before their grandma's wooden box was lowered into the grave.

- Candles held by special friends were used to form a sort of "honour guard" as pallbearers took my sister's casket out of the chapel. Candles symbolize Jesus as Light of the World.

- Flowers are left for remembrance. Long-stemmed red roses placed on the casket by family mourners, individualize their relationship to the deceased before the funeral service.

I once bought a casket saddle and built the spray of flowers for an uncle who was Saskatchewan born. The tiger lilies, palm grasses, wheat and flax were appropriate for my grieving farming relatives. You might be surprised to discover the simplicity desired for a simple clutch of roses and fern by loved ones.

- Music may be sacred or secular. "Great is Thy Faithfulness" seems to be our family favourite. We all smiled when our niece belted out "God Is in Control," a contemporary piece with a strong, comforting message. Singing a familiar song around the graveside soothes the circle of healing.

- Grave markers can be placed when the grieving family is ready. Our family's grave stones bear the signature of the deceased to personalize it. You can learn a lot just by studying the grave markers in a cemetery. We took a family photo of the clan surrounding the headstone.

- We used the children's drawings of angels and messages of love in grandma's casket to help them communicate their feelings of loss. Mourning is a process, and there are many ways to mark a loved one's passing.

Helping Children Deal with Loss and Grief
February 2001

We should have seen that the stoical faces and silent voices spoke loudly of loss and pain. In our sincere attempts to accept mother's death, we overprotected the little ones and denied them the opportunity to grieve," writes Doreen Reimer Peters, author of *Helping Children Deal with Loss and Grief.*

Peters wrote her handbook for families and caregivers dealing with divorce and death. The death of an animal, family member, or loss of a parent through divorce needs to be grieved. "It is very important to realize that although a child may not seem to be grieving, the experience of loss is real and must be taken seriously."

"With every change there is a loss, with every loss there is grief. Anger and grief go together, so give yourself permission to mourn," adds Dr. Nikki Gerrard, psychologist and counsellor. "Support each other."

In the book *Helping Children Grieve: When Someone They Love Dies* Sandra Fox writes that there are three important tasks:

1. **Understanding** – knowing what death or separation mean.

2. **Grieving** – feeling the feelings and working through them.

3. **Commemorating** – honouring and keeping alive the memory of the person who has died or who is gone.

Should young children go to the funeral home? Yes, if they are prepared for what they will see, who will be there, how people may be feeling and what they will be doing. Our children were different in how they wanted to say goodbye to their grandparent; one was comfortable touching Grandma's hand, the other stood quietly back at a distance after writing Grandma a letter.

Going to the funeral home:

- Provides structure for early grieving. "If the opportunity of participating in the mourning rites is denied children they are unable to experience concretely the fact of death, and they will be left with an unresolved situation," says family therapist Claudia Jewett, author of *Helping Children Cope with Separation and Loss*. The funeral allows the child to see that many other people share in his sorrow and love for the lost person. If the child is shut out of these services, he experiences damaging, scary feelings that he must have done something wrong.

- Helps bring a sense of closure; the funeral marks that a change has taken place.

- Provides a place to vent emotions and receive support from family and friends. It allows the child to feel sad and show their grief by crying.

- Includes the child so she doesn't feel angry or left out. "If children are ignored by the adults closest to them when a death occurs, another caring adult should step in to give the appropriate help" says Peters.

Attending the funeral or memorial service helps provide needed rituals for children. But children of any age should not be forced to participate. Remembering the loved one's birthday and reviewing photos and keepsakes, or a visit to the graveside later may be helpful.

Although children of varying ages have differences, we need to:

- Share information at the child's level of understanding. Word pictures like a rose bud, blooming, petals falling, and the flower fading may help you explain death. "When faith in God is part of a family's experience, make sure the loss is explained in terms of a loving God," says Peters. "First the fact of death and the pain of separation need to be faced and acknowledged. Then talking about heaven can be comforting."

- Talk about and accept feelings. "Much of the outcome of a child's loss or separation experience hinges on how adults allow and even encourage the child to accept his strong feelings about what has happened," notes Jewett.

- Be available for ongoing discussions; mourning is a process. Admit that you do not have all the answers. Make an extra effort to reassure the child of your love and acceptance. Keep routines. Talk to the child's teacher about the loss. Drawing, writing, playing with puppets, and lighting candles are activities that help express feelings.

- Share information in small amounts at a time. Let the child know that it is okay to be angry. The best way to deal with the anger is to talk about it.

- Allow silence for awhile, but observe the child to see if the loss is unresolved. Professional help may be needed if the child continues to be unresponsive.

Our communities will be healthier and stronger if we learn to support each other as we grieve, and learn to live with the reality of death.

CHAPTER 13

GRADUATION

GRADUATES: BUNDLES OF POTENTIAL
JUNE 2000

Twenty-two years ago as a valedictorian I encouraged my peers to use their potential to reach out to people. The words still ring true today.

"We can be sensitive to people as individuals with special needs. Communication is vital.

We must be ourselves, and honest with others, taking time to listen and hearing with an inner ear. Our knowledge is power. Power to put programs and people into action. We will learn and develop our potential in the process. Hopefully we will learn quickly from our mistakes and have the energy and motivation to persevere towards new challenges and ideas."

A deep love of learning for a lifetime is what I hope the grads of 2000 are embracing.

Learning to accept their unique gifts and personalities with all the inherent potential. Leading others with principle-based leadership. Lovingly assured of God's love, which gives their life meaning and the desire to be a "giver."

Teens today are looking for anchors because so much of their family life is transient, and technological change is constant. My grad speech included the song " I am a promise, I am a possibility, I am a promise with a capital P, I am a great big bundle of potentiality. I am learning to hear God's voice, and I am trying to make the right choice, I am a promise to be anything God wants me to be."

We all want to be loved. Teens may choose to find friendships in groups of young people developing lifelong friendships based on common values. These teens do not bolster their self-esteem with "I have a boyfriend or girlfriend", they're waiting to develop their interests before dating when they feel ready for an intimate, committed lifelong relationship.

I always hated it when as a graduate, people would say, "Well, Elaine, what are you going to do with the rest of your life?" I encourage grads to take one day, one month or one year at a time, basing their decisions on sound Biblical principles and strong character. God speaks to us through the small still voice of the Holy Spirit by other believers, His word, our circumstances and through prayer.

We are bundles of potentiality. Support a graduate with strong words of loving acceptance and the promise of your prayers. Be there to listen, to challenge the myths of a society that chooses not to follow God's guidelines. Offer hope and encouragement to plan goals that will give young people a true sense of meaning and happiness in their lives.

ROOTS AND WINGS
JUNE 1995

"Lost time is never found again." – Benjamin Franklin

The summer goes by quickly, the kids grow like weeds, and in few short years they graduate into life. This summer I challenge you to think of how you can give your family "roots" and "wings."

Roots are the things to which we hold fast to create strong family bonds and connections ... and to ground us. Wings are the times when we let go of things to create a strong sense of independence ... and to fly.

Plant "roots" by holding fast to the principles that guide your life. This summer might be a great time to create a list of life principles to talk about at the breakfast table or around a campfire. Here are a few examples: A wise person learns from the mistakes of others. What I feed my mind will determine how I think. How I think will determine how I live. God is always nearer to me than anything or anyone else. We can all be kind and courteous.

Plan family fun time with a list of inexpensive or free things to do. Your goals can be in writing with headings for learning (intellectual), living (physical pursuits), loving (emotional and social growth) and leaving a legacy (spiritual goals). Our family hopes to read, hike, camp, and picnic, celebrate a 50th wedding anniversary, and invite friends over for supper. The kids will also learn some new swimming skills, how to tell time, and learn to tie shoelaces!

Creative time and care is needed to make good family memories happen. Give your children what they desperately want and only you can give, yourself. Record the fun events of summer in scrapbooks, photos, videos and with family storytelling. Talk about expectations for fun as a family; don't exceed what is realistic for your family. If every kid in town is getting a new trampoline and yours aren't, that is okay!

The "wings" part of parenting requires letting go to create opportunities for children to develop independence. Going to camp is a great way for kids to test being away from home in a fun environment. Let go of your fears of what might happen; pray for God's provision and protection. My years at camp as a camper and counsellor have had a great impact on my spiritual growth, and leadership abilities. Go to camp as a family, too!

Let go of financial worries that block you from creating fun family times. Fun doesn't have to cost a fortune or stress your operating loans to the limit. Brainstorm with your family for ideas. If we roast marshmallows around a campfire, the kids tell us they have had a great summer!

Vacate your daily routine. Yes, the steers or hogs have to be fed. But then look at the map and draw a 100-kilometre circle around your town. You have lots of options for day trips to fairs, swinging bridges, lakes or places to hike and explore. What about seeing some long-lost cousins? Loosen up on your need to be orderly, clean and organized.

Simple things can be fun. Giving your children roots and wings takes some creative planning. Grandparents can give lots of wisdom and time to their sons, daughters and grandkids. Someone once said, "It is not where you go in life that matters. It is who you're with."

BEER, BEING THERE AND BOUNDARIES
JULY 2001

A lot of teens can't separate fun from being plastered" writes a frustrated teen on an internet message board. Summer time is drinking time for some teens with lots of free time and the lame excuse of being bored! I know teens who mountain bike, camp, work, help others, build cabins, and do lots of fun stuff without beer, but why are teens drinking?

If you punch "why teens drink alcohol" into your computer's search engine, you might be surprised at the results:

- **Pleasure:** alcohol is a powerful drug and changes the way you feel. Kids are discovering that beer can medicate their pain as they seek pleasant sensations at low blood alcohol levels. "It helps me relax and unwind after a stressful day!" What are you modeling as a parent, do you need caffeine to get you started, wine at supper, and a pill to help you sleep? Exercise is a good stress reliever. Walk!

- **Easy to rebel:** Drinking beer makes some kids feel grown-up, especially if they can do something illegal in the company of friends. Peer pressure factors in here. It's a fast way to gain acceptance to a group or "act cool." Experimenting with booze is likely if the parents drink and if parents don't have clear rules about drinking.

- **Media:** Messages in today's lyrics, videos and lifestyles imply that drinking is glamourous and exciting. The real message teens are missing is that "you don't have to drink to have fun!"

- **Depression:** Many more teens are depressed than families realize, because people are not telling the truth or talking clearly about what is really happening in their lives. Nearly all kids will tell their parents they don't drink. If there is a history of depression or problem drinking in your family, get a physician's opinion. Treat your teen's brain right and check out that raging hormone or chemical balance! If you have a problem, don't drink it away, tell someone. Don't use booze as an escape from reality.

- **Easy to get beer and get drunk:** Our local paper's RCMP report tells of a 16-year-old charged with impaired driving and being released to his parents. People supply booze to under age kids or leave the house unattended for long periods of time. In a Students Against Drunk Driving (SADD) survey in the U.S., 29 per cent of the teens said the reason they drink is "to get drunk!" Bush parties are toxic when kids drink to excess and are at high risk for alcohol poisoning, date rape, and death in a car accident. Getting drunk sucks!

Why I don't drink

When I was in high school I was very involved in sports and getting good marks to help finance my university. I loved to have fun with friends at dances, but I refused to destroy my valuable brain cells, and let myself be pushed around by guys who might try to take advantage of me if I was drinking. I didn't need beer to have fun, and I still don't. In college I had a Friday night group that had 100 people who loved to sing, study, go camping, play touch football and eat ice cream at the Bridge Drive Inn. We knew how to socialize and support each other. However, the clincher for my anger against drunk driving came on New Year's Eve when my best friend was in a coma after being hit by a drunk – a person was dead. Then my sister was killed by a drunk driver at age 23. She was beautiful, inside and out; our family never really recovered from missing her. Her friend told me recently that her death made him so angry that he continues to pull car keys from guys who are too drunk to drive.

BE THERE

Parents need to invest tons of loving time and energy into the lives of their kids. You need to know what is happening in their lives and who their real friends are. Show nurturing guidance and explain why you don't drink. Talk about why you follow the guidelines you live by.

Let them know you are always only a phone call away, even in the middle of the night. You will come rescue them from a bad situation, or you will let them say, "My mom and dad would kill me if I was drinking...no thanks!"

Teens listen to their friends opinions, so let your home be a haven for their friends. Don't let other adults provide booze to your kids. An adult may take 10 years to develop an alcohol problem, but the metabolism and growth rate of a teen gives him the chance to be an alcoholic in 10 months! Yikes!

Help your teen build good social skills by doing lots of different things and promoting healthy group activities. Problem drinkers are emotionally stuck, like little children inside a big person's body. Encourage your child to do volunteer work and feel good by helping others.

Set boundaries. "What part of 'No' do you not understand?" Are there consequences for drinking and lying? Set clear and realistic expectations for getting good grades at school and staying on school teams. Tell teens to intervene when friends are in trouble with excessive drinking. If my daughter was getting drunk and you knew about it and didn't tell me, I would be extremely angry.

Make it clear that under-age drinking, and driving under the influence are against the law and against your family rules. Alcohol abuse makes me angry. I encourage you to talk with and really listen to the teens in your life. Teenage drinking is everybody's problem. It's just not cool.

PONDER AND PLANT:

Who are the young people in your life who could use some hope in their lives? _____

_____

_____

_____

_____

_____

_____

_____

_____

_____

_____

_____

_____

_____

_____

_____

_____

_____

CHAPTER 14

HARVEST

Filling Harvest's Emotional Tank
August 2000

"Store up for yourselves treasures in heaven, where moth and rust do not destroy. For where your treasure is, there your heart will be also." – Matthew 6:20

Last month our family drove to Detriot Lakes, Minnesota to experience a Christian music festival "Spiritfest Midwest," a weekend of our favourite musicians, camping, and encouragement. As we drove, I was amused how farm families used various forms of art to express their sense of humour.

A carved tree stump was painted to look like Moses extending his arm. A large bronze iron rooster was perched along the field to watch the Interstate traffic. A smiling dog face painted on a huge rock at the end of a driveway greeted visitors. Someone stuffed the tail-end of their plane into the header of a combine – a harvest accident we will all avoid!

The most comforting piece of art work was on the bank of a well-cut ditch, "Jesus Cares" lettered with white rocks along Highway #59.

Harvest is always a time of great expectations mixed with bitter disappointment or happy surprises. Some of you got the rain, some still ache to see grain that has withered away from lack of moisture. Whatever the state of your crops, there will be a harvest. It's a tough time for farm families if they have taken time to get the combine ready, fueled and full of grain, but the people running those powerful machines have neglected to keep their emotional tank full.

In 1985, we cut open a gorgeous crop of flax with the straight-header. I was so blessed and thankful that I could be driving and helping with harvest. The harvest of 1984 I had been hospitalized, so good health was a blessing. When you've been really sick, your priorities change. Harvest is hectic, but relationships are key, and need to be nurtured in stressful times. Here's my "E" list of ways to keep your emotional tank full:

- **Embrace:** Take 60 seconds to give a firm hug to your spouse before you hit the fields. Hugs are good for the hemoglobin; you'll feel better when you know you are loved, even when you plug the combine!

- **Elevate your legs:** Take time to rest, 10 minutes when you're feeling sluggish, and get to bed for at least six hours! Keeping up your nighttime sleep will prevent accidents and foolish downtime.

- **Explain:** While there is dew on the ground, let the family and other workers know what the plan is for the day. A few minutes spent in making sure everyone knows the expectation for the day will help keep harvest humming instead of fuming! When things go wrong, count to 10 before you vent your frustrations.

- **Eat:** Your body can't run well on empty, so nourish it with good food and snacks. There is time to eat your supper in the swaths on the tailgate of the truck with your kids.

- **Encourage one another:** Mistakes happen, but how you handle them will groom the next generation to handle farming, or convince them they can't take the hassle. A positive mental attitude is the key ingredient of a smooth functioning emotional tank. It is wise to not make assumptions, and make sure your instructions are understood.

- **Emit thankfulness:** Some swaths will be bountiful, some will be a disappointment, but you will eat, be clothed, and sheltered this winter. Matthew 16:26 puts material things into perspective: "What good will it be for a man if he gains the whole world, yet forfeits his soul?" Our relationship with God and our family is what really counts.

Keep your headers up in the low spots, and keep your heads to fill the emotional tanks of those you harvest with! Blessings to you all for a good harvest.

LIFE IS LIKE A COMBINE
AUGUST 2003

Harvest is a favourite time of year. As a combine driver, I join the excitement of bringing in the crop as efficiently as possible. I enjoy long hours of solitude on the field, with lots of time to ponder what's happening in our family and life in general. This is the picture when the crops are evenly ripe, dry, and the weather is cooperating. There are also the loud "thunks" when the header plugs, or the frustration of catching a clump of mud, but usually things get back into the flow.

Plugging the combine is a great metaphor for resistance. You can't push too much too fast through the powerful machine. Farm people are going through tremendous changes again this year with new challenges, and we get frustrated when our family doesn't want what we want.

Why don't you want what I want? is Rick Maurer's practical book on working through three levels of resistance. Level 1: "I don't get it"; Level 2: "I don't like it"; and Level 3: "I don't trust you." Maurer believes we can muster support for our ideas without hard sell, manipulation or power plays. He encourages readers to stay engaged with the person ... seek understanding, favourable reactions, and develop trust.

I've experienced resistance to change in farm families when I've tried to present too many ideas for change too quickly. Things plug up fast when people aren't given time to see the same picture we see. "When people are afraid they will lose something important, when their fear response kicks in...their emotional brain takes over and limits their ability to stay engaged with us,"says Maurer.

Smooth combine operators make sure they feed the machine with a good consistent speed, checking the monitors. We need to check our understanding with our families, planting seeds of change gradually, and paying attention to emotional monitors.

Beeping in the tractor cab alerts us to problems. What alerts us in our conversations that we are really getting it, and listening to the other person's viewpoints? Do they understand? Are they reacting negatively or positively? Is there sufficient trust between us for them to support us?

Maurer suggests six principles of engagement to help move through resistance:

1. **Know your intention:** Focus on issues instead of positions. The key intention of combining is to put all the grain in the tank, and not leave a trail of grain on the ground! The issue is trusting the person who sets the sieves, and checking the tank and the trail behind you. If you are intending to make changes in your farm family, have you developed the trust you need for support?

2. **Consider the context.** The focus of getting the crop off sets the context , other things are lower priority. Time your conversations well, consider where they are taking place, and the quality of the relationship. People in harvest are focused on that priority. Maybe you've been trying to make changes with people who are just too tired to think or change!

3. **Avoid knee jerk reactions.** Slamming the hydrostatic lever can put your face in the windshield of your combine. Similarly, you need to know your triggers or "hot buttons" in conversations and avoid them. Your goal is to seek understanding and build commitment.

4. **Pay attention.** When a cutting knife breaks, you get a trail of grain heads standing – evidence that you need to stop and

change the broken part. Do you listen to others to be changed? Do you care about what the other person has to say? Make time for feedback. Listen. Be willing to be influenced by what you hear.

5. **Explore deeply.** Messing around with the concaves is exploring deeply into the guts of the combine. You hope you don't have to do this in the field, but it happens. People are afraid of the unknown, that is why farmers resist talking about a different way of working or living off the farm. Families need to find a safe way to talk and explore possibilities for common ground. Maurer says you know when you have explored enough when the person shifts from "you to us," and it feels like a weight has just lifted.

6. **Find ways to connect.** When my trucker comments that I am cutting too high, I make adjustments, and don't steam with the criticism. The real concern is to do a great job, and not leave too much straw for the cultivator to handle. Maurer's process for people to connect is to identify the real fear or concern.

State what is important to you. Then, turn that statement of concern into a statement of what you both want. For example, a farm spouse may say, "I am afraid that we are not making decisions about our life off the farm yard, and that is impacting our children's decisions. It is important to me that we have a plan for our new home, and the way we will continue to work. We both want to stay involved, and find a way to live in harmony with our working children."

As a Farm Family Coach I am deeply committed to helping farm families work through the hard issues and choices that face them. Visit Maurer's website at www.beyondresistance.com. Have a great harvest!

Tips to Make Harvest Happier
August 2004

"People just can't be expected to work '24/7.' It's no wonder he can't keep a hired man!" These are the comments of top farmers from Pike Management Group's summer conference. I had great fun speaking to Canadian and Australian farmers about farm help concerns. I use two hats with index card labels. One hat is the BOSS, and one is MANAGER. We have to make an intentional choice about our approach with our employees. Harvest is the crucible of communication strengths and weaknesses.

Here's my encouragement for managing a happier harvest:

- **COMMUNICATION:** A BOSS says: "It's my way or the highway. I don't have time to mess around with your ideas."
  A MANAGER says: "Tell me more about … what height you think we should cut at and why. This is our plan for which crops we'll harvest first. Keep me posted with your radio or cell phone."

- **WORK ETHIC:** A BOSS says: "We work all the time because the most important thing is money, I'll just pay you more. There's no time for fun or family, there's too much work to do."
  A MANAGER says: " We work smart as a team. When it rains we'll have a rest, and my shift workers are thrilled they only need to show up here five days a week! Let's all enjoy a special supper together to celebrate the end of harvest."

- **POWER, CONTROL AND DECISIONS:** A BOSS says: "I own this combine so listen to me. I'll make the final decision and tell you what I decide."
  A MANAGER says: "Some decisions are like leaves on a tree. You have the skills to make a lot of decisions without my input. Make a decision and act on it. For the bigger decisions, talk to me before you take action."

- **TRAINING AND LEARNING:** A BOSS says: "Man! He's been he's been watching me run this place for 5 years, he should just know what to do! He should figure how out to set the grain monitor and the sieves on his own!"
  A MANAGER says: "I'm glad we took lots of time getting the combines ready. Everyone understands how to use the new monitors, and they feel okay about asking for help when things don't work right. Our goal is to teach, learn and let go, so that everyone gains more skills. We try to minimize mistakes like forgetting to put the gas cap back on after fueling the combine. We watch out for each other."

- **HELPFUL SYSTEMS:** A BOSS says: "We just don't have time to keep track of each truck's weight off the field." "Take that paperwork to town and let them figure it out! I don't want to spend time keeping track of work hours or wading through that manual!"
  A MANAGER says: " I thought these systems that we've put in place will help us measure what we need to change. It just takes a few extra minutes to weigh the trucks, and document the harvest conditions. I've always felt that if you can't measure it, you can't change it!"

- **GRATITUDE:** A BOSS says: "I don't have time to stop and eat a hot meal. Sandwiches for eight weeks helps me eat on the run. I'm not as young as I used to be, but I can still keep myself running hard during harvest. I expect you to work just like me. Your paycheque should be thanks enough."
  A MANAGER says: "Let me trade off while you have a decent supper and a short break. I'd rather have the combines running smoothly with no errors, than deal with the costly downtime when operator fatigue sets in. You're doing a great job, and I really appreciate your good harvest habits. You are careful to check that you're not throwing grain out the back, or missing strips."

I love harvest. In 2003, it was early, hot and very smooth. Already we sense that 2004 will be late and long. Each year brings new challenges, but keep in mind that the people on your farm are your most important asset. Think about the ways you can intentionally manage a happier harvest this year. All the best to you as you keep those combines humming. I hope you're humming, too!

GAINS IN THE RAIN
AUGUST 1999

"Normal is only a setting on your clothes dryer!"
– author unknown

We are not having a "normal" year. We farm in southwestern Manitoba where the showers of blessing turned to a deluge of more than 14" of rain during the seeding season. Too much rain, and watching the potential for income gain go down the drain can be frustrating.

It was no accident that I found Phil Callaway's book *Making Life Rich Without Any Money* for my husband. For myself, I bought *No Rain No Gain Devotions to Guide You Through The Storms of Life* by Susan Lenkes.

As I write this, it's mid-June, and we are still seeding. I'm thankful we can get 90 acres out of a quarter. I'm thrilled my brother and his wide-tired tractor, and packer-less air seeder are here to help. I encourage you to take some time to lift the spirits of friends and family in Manitoba and Saskatchewan who are looking at a sea of green weeds with little or no crop.

Dig deep and cultivate a grateful heart. My house didn't get bombed last night, and there was ample food on the table. Callaway's book inspired me to make a list of things I was thankful for on May 31st. For those of you who have always wanted to read someone's diary, here's a peek at my journal:

I am loved by God, adopted as an heir in Christ. I have good health, and am getting in better shape. I am loved by a husband who is kind, consistent, and a good provider. He has time to coach ball and watch his son in a track meet today.

Our son hugged and kissed me after his prayers. I am appreciated by a teenage girl who thought her mom was cool enough to be the band trip chaperon. Now ready to catch up on sleep! I am the recipient of a hand-painted black skillet by a budding artist and stalled gardener. She received my perennials with joy. Given red flax seed by our loyal employee who wishes he could be seeding, but can't due to extreme wet. Watching birds land on the Thunderchild crab tree I've planted in memory of my mom, my gardening mentor, whom I miss. An offer of equipment to sow by my brother. Feeling the fresh breeze and listening to the wind in the trees as I walk down my lane and observe the ducks skimming the water in the ditches and a field of drowned oats! Being thankful that this list is not exhaustive ... and this is just one day.

Pull your neighbours out. Rainy days and stuck tractors are great opportunities to link-up with your farming neighbours and town friends. We made history in early June at the ball game with all the guys and gals from Caranton corner watching their daughters play. Prayer chains (people calling another to pray) for sunshine, and support to hurting families are always in season.

Connect all circuits, make the call. We received phone calls from city friends, and farmers who knew we were getting too much rain. Perhaps you can afford a few words of encouragement over the phone line to a farm family you suspect is like a dry well, needing to be filled with caring and kind words.

Check fluid and fuel levels, share a meal. We can be rich in relationships when we invite people to share their hearts with

"Though the fig tree does not bud and there are no grapes on the vines, though the olive crop fails and the fields produce no food, though there are no sheep in the pen and no cattle in the stalls, yet I will rejoice in the Lord, I will be joyful in God my Saviour. The Sovereign Lord is my strength; he makes my feet like the feet of a deer, he enables me to go on the heights." – Habakkuk 3: 17-19, NIV

us over a good meal. Our town friends watched the skies with us, and had us over for supper.

Know the signs of wear and tear. Sleeplessness, irritability, aching body parts, lack of appetite, may be signs of a depression looming. Get professional help from your doctor, and don't put it off! There are many different reasons for depression. Extremely stressful circumstances may set it off; deal with it. Embrace the people whose family member is suffering. Don't avoid them.

Read your manual. I believe God is in control. His words in the Bible promise that He is always with us, no matter what. Know you are loved by God and He cares for you. Farming is a tough challenge, but God will be with you through it all. Watch the sky. Nurture your soul. Get rid of the weeds in your life that are pulling you down. The harvest will come.

CHAPTER 15

THANKSGIVING

How to Cultivate A Grateful Heart
October 1997

"A faithful heart is treasure found
It rises up from sacred ground
Its precious light consumes the dark
'Cause love shines bright from a faithful heart."
– by Jamie Houston and Jim Jacobson

As my hungry rotary combine was swallowing up an ample golden wheat swath, I sat humming ,"a grateful heart is treasure found. " My transposed lyrics of the above song helped pass the hours of reaping what we had sown. My visits to the elevator for moisture tests revealed it was best to simply say "I'm thankful for the crop we have in the bin." I didn't want to discuss exact yields, because the crop's bounty varied greatly depending on where and when the rains nourished or diseased them!

As farmers we have a tangible example every harvest of ways to be thankful. It's easy to be thankful when the hopper fills quickly, but how can one cultivate a grateful heart when the bins of life are not overflowing?

Our well of thankfulness needs to be filled on a daily basis. I suppose that is why Sarah Ban Breathnach's book, *Simple*

Abundance, is such a bestseller. She encourages practicing the "practical principle of gratitude" urging us to keep a daily gratitude journal.

Could you list five things at the end of each day that you are thankful for?

My sister-in-law asks her children each night at bedtime to tell her what they are thankful for that day. Your family could start a similar tradition using two wheat kernels or sunflower seeds on an empty plate to spark thankfulness thoughts at the dinner table – as the plate is passed around each person shares something he or she is grateful for from the past year.

After a tough harvest with disappointing yields, can you be thankful for your daily bread, that your basic needs are still being met? With an attitude of thankfulness for the quality of life we enjoy on the prairies, with wonderful listening, supportive friends, let's look down the road and enjoy the beautiful sunset.

In the twilight years of life, take time to share loving and grateful moments with your family. Those memories will sustain them though the tough times of "letting go" later on. The things I'm thankful for this year are:

- an abiding faith nourished by a loving God and family of believers who support one another in practical ways and with prayer.

- good health. An acquaintance fighting breast cancer really puts this into perspective. We all need to take care of our physical and emotional self.

- spirited, lively children. Their unique personalities and boundless energy are a blessing. Hey, stubbornness may translate to perseverance in adulthood ! Hug your teen today!

- hope for the life beyond. Each day is a gift. As my father-in-law's vitality is gradually slipping away, I'm thankful for his love, faith, and hope in eternal rest.

- an average harvest. Hailstorms, drought, disease are part of our farming lot in life. The tough years teach us empathy

> *"Do not be anxious about anything, but in everything, by prayer and petition, with thanksgiving, present your requests to God. And the peace of God, which transcends all understanding, will guard your hearts and your minds in Christ Jesus."*
> – Phillipians 4:6,7

for our neighbour's outcomes, with tactful sharing of "yield comparisons at the local elevator or coffee shop."

- a loving husband, who is a great father. Let's celebrate marriage and parenting!

Keep cultivating your grateful heart, it will be treasure found.

PUT MORE THAN TURKEY ON THE MENU
OCTOBER 2002

Harvest is a bit of a battle this year, with frequent showers and 4-wheel drive tractors ready to pull out mucky combines. But...we are thankful...we have a crop. The bottom line of the farm business is making a profit, the money to keep a operation thriving. The bottom line of ownership is to have power and control over the land, herd, or equipment that your farm needs.

What is the bottom line of a family? If you answered "LOVE"... congratulations, you're on the right track. "The Bermuda triangle of complex farm family businesses is family(love), ownership(power) and business (money)," says Dr. John Fast, founder and former director of the Centre for Family Business at the University of Waterloo. He says the definition of success for farm families is having everyone come home at Christmas (or Thanksgiving) to eat turkey. Farm families that are healthy and strong, know how to celebrate together, and they want to be together.

When you deeply value your family you make the effort to show appreciation. Fast calls mothers the CEO – "Chief

Emotional Officer"– of the family. Mom is the one who monitors feelings, identity, appreciation and recognition. She makes sure that the stuffing, favourite salads, and pie is on the menu for Thanksgiving. She hopes that everyone will come to the table as an adult, with the ability to make genuine choices about their futures as part of the farm family business, or not.

Wait, I thought we were talking about celebrating Thanksgiving. Well yes, but the problem is that in farm families you are family, business partners, children, employees, in-laws … and maybe a prodigal son or daughter.

We all have many roles, and Fast says that sometimes we forget which hat we are wearing, and the roles get confused. This Thanksgiving, wear your family hat, and make an effort to show love and appreciation.

Drought, grasshoppers, selling off prized herds, and a multititude of other stresses may have you wondering what you have to be thankful about this year. Come to the table prepared to bless the other members of your family with your presence and love.

Say a prayer of thanks for the circle of love and nurturing that you have experienced. Commit to celebrating the things in life that foul weather and tough times cannot steal – your love for one another.

Let everyone say just one thing they are thankful for, and if they are too choked up to speak … just say "pass." I've had phone calls from some readers who feel like the walking wounded when it comes to their family relationships. Sharing fun and food around the table can be the starting point of re-building trust, laughter, and comfort.

Communication, communication, communication and forgiveness are the four ingredients that are critical factors for success, Dr. Fast adds. Put love and appreciation with thankfulness on your Thanksgiving menu this year. Count your blessings, and leave the counting of your net worth or retirement fund for another day.

Here is my Thanksgiving prayer: "May our family be filled with loving-kindness as we reflect on all the good gifts that God has provided for us. We are blessed to live in this country of freedom, and to make a living from the land. Help us not to take one another for granted, and show our love in many ways. Each day is a gift. Thank you Lord. Amen."

TEARS WITH THE TURKEY
OCTOBER 2003

Though the fig tree does not bud and there are no grapes on the vines, though the olive crop fails and the fields produce no food, though there are no sheep in the pen and no cattle in the stalls, yet I will rejoice in the Lord , I will be joyful in God my Saviour. - Habakkuk 3:17-18

"Habakkuk teaches us that joy is not dependent on circumstances but can be embraced at the worst of times," writes Mike Mason in *Champagne for the Soul*. Mason says that happiness doesn't just happen, it is an act of the will. As I read Mason's 90-day experiment in joy, I was deeply encouraged by the changes in his life as he chose joy.

Mason married a college friend of mine, and it was great to see how he felt his melancholy character was deeply changed by joy.

Can we as farmers also choose to be thankful in a year when there are too many cattle in the stalls? There are grain piles on neighbours' fields, but in yours the grasshoppers have left nothing. The sheep are in the pen also, because politics beyond your control have stymied your ability to market your livestock. To say the year has been tough is an understatement for many.

Farm families look for stability, security and control of their affairs. With the triple blow of drought, grasshoppers and BSE (Bovine Spongioform Encephalopathy), how can one choose to be thankful? Thankfulness is a choice. In a year like 2003, it may require several steps taken in the same direction to count our blessings.

At our Foodgrains Bank harvest this year my friend relayed her feelings about listening to a B.C. rancher describe how her husband herded out the cows just in time, and as they turned back to look, they silently watched the ranch go up in flames. I had heard the same broadcast with the identical reaction as my friend. We both cried.

Tears of pain flow with empathy for families who are suffering great loss, and pain this fall. We also listen to reports of bombings and war ravaged regions that seem far away. Are we thankful to live in a country of peace?

This morning a cattleman friend called with an offer of beef for my freezer. Producers are buoyed with the support of consumers who have shown their support with their stomachs. Be thankful that we've made a connection of goodwill with some folk.

The financial squeeze really has no easy answers. The bottom line is summed up by Dr. Nikki Gerrard's response to a financially-strained farmer: "I can't save your farm, but I can help you save your family." Gerrard spent 12 years helping Saskatchewan communities be proactive in dealing with farm stress.

Have you told your family that you love and appreciate them? A radio report says that tears flow from a 60-year-old cattleman under financial duress. Yes, cowboys do cry; and I'm glad to hear they know the healing power of tears. Vulnerability is not a trait farmers and ranchers like to show openly; they are usually a proud, independent, self-sufficient bunch.

Now is not the time to hold back from your family. Your spouse needs to feel and know the security and commitment of the relationship, no matter how tough things are. Farm families need to know is it okay to ask for help from outside resources, and talk, listen and talk some more. People feel isolated when the stress is high. Invite your neighbour over for conversation and coffee. Be courageous enough to make the invitation and walk alongside them in their crisis.

I heard a story of an oil-rigger sending money home to the farm to help the cash flow. Non-farm family members have a great role to play in supporting the family back on the ranch. Be thankful for the roots and wings your farm family gave you. Bless your family with your prayers, calls and cash.

I once kept a gratitude journal for a whole year, each night noting five things for which I was thankful. This was a soothing activity for me when my mother was dying, when I could consciously look for things to be grateful for, even when grieving a loss.

God's word, the Bible, is a huge love letter to us of His faithfulness. We are secure knowing that we are deeply loved by God, and He cares for us all the time. It is my prayer that you will encounter believers to encourage you, pray with you, and be a practical help to you this Thanksgiving. Give thanks with a grateful heart around the turkey or beef this year.

PONDER AND PLANT:

What's your fondest Thanksgiving celebration memory? _____

_____

_____

_____

_____

_____

_____

_____

_____

What seeds of thankfulness are you going to sow this year? ____

_____

_____

_____

_____

_____

CREATIVE HOSPITALITY
SEPTEMBER 1998

Perhaps this Thanksgiving you'll have the chance to open your hearts and home to strangers, someone just passing through who needs to be at your table. Before you start worrying about the food and how your house looks, remember that hospitality is defined as "entertaining guests with kindness and liberality."

I grew up in a home where unexpected guests were served with graciousness and warmth, no matter what was on the table. I've served grape punch to the vice-president of a large banking firm, and fruit and Arrowroot biscuits when guests just happened by.

Don't fret about everything being perfect before you invite guests into your home. If you've had a tough harvest, you likely need to share the load with friends around a campfire with wieners and lemonade. We've had great times visiting around the fire in summer and in the middle of December! Our friends are a large family who celebrates the end of harvest with huge bonfire!

Good manners are nothing more than making the other person feel at ease. Your positive gracious attitude is the key to creative hospitality. Karen Burton Mains, author of *Open Heart Open Home*, offers these suggestions:

- **Never clean before company.** Mains cleans on her schedule, not for people. I give the bathroom a quick check, but dust and Lego on the floor don't stop me from having company. Someone once admitted she felt uncomfortable having me over, because the drapes didn't match the carpet! People are longing for relationship, color schemes shouldn't be a barrier to hospitality! Take a risk and vacuum after the party!

- **Do things with flair!** Candles lit in the room, a quilt for a tablecloth, or a buffet of "clean out the fridge" is fine! Our crock pot simmers lentil or pea soup for guests. They are glad to be welcomed into our home and don't expect a six-course gourmet dinner! On one occasion, friends in Calgary took the time to research the meaning of our names, each placecard noted the guest's name along with its meaning. We felt special!

- **Do as much preparation ahead of time as possible.** Keep track of menu ideas that work like simple desserts and soups with bread. Let children learn from you, stuffing glasses with cloth napkins, and setting a fun table.

- **Clean as you go.** Mains has a system of dealing with dishes as she entertains. Personally, some of my best visiting happens around the kitchen sink at clean-up time. Hot-dogs and cocoa around the campfire requires little clean-up at all!

- **Use all the help that comes your way.** Our former Bible study group had a wonderful way of doing celebrations "potluck" style. Accept your guest's queries of "What can I bring?" with gratefulness. The "bring-a-pie" night is traditionally a big hit at our Thanksgiving gathering in our church, it works for home parties, too.

When one of my friends turned 40, she used the dinner party gathering to bless her friends. Each guest was told what his or her friendship and lifestyle meant to her. We will all remember her words of encouragement and hospitality.

If words are hard for you to share, use the comfort of great food shared with family and friends. It seems that good fellowship around food tends to open people's mouths and hearts. Take time to share the things you are thankful for this year! Don't put off having company ... be a blessing to your guests.

CHAPTER 16

GIFTS

THE GIFT OF ENCOURAGEMENT
DECEMBER 1994

"A word aptly spoken is like apples of gold in settings of silver." – Proverbs 25:11

The most precious gifts I've received have been gifts of words. As a farm woman who witnessed the devastating work of hail and tornado-like winds during a recent harvest, I'm thankful for friends who gave me the gift of encouragement.

The gift of words is not easily shared. I once asked my mother to give me a letter for my birthday telling me what hopes she had for me as a child, and to recall meaningful childhood memories. She found it easier to buy me a beautiful wind-suit with matching earrings that year. But the encouraging words were later documented in a hard-cover journal, in which Mom spent an entire winter making entries and giving responses to questions. Perhaps you have a notebook, scrapbook or journal waiting to be filled with loving memories and words for your family.

What kind of words? Your words may be words of comfort and cheer; they may be words of strength and affirmation. Mark Twain once said, "A man can live for two months on one good compliment." Possibly you can also encourage with words of instruction.

A word of encouragement can make the difference between giving up or going on. You might like to start a file or scrapbook of letters or notes that people have given you. My file is bright pink, and easily found! On days that your emotional bank account is "in the red" an encouraging word can balance the account again.

For the price of a stamp, an envelope and some pretty paper, you can communicate value and worth to your family and friends. My friend, a mother of three young girls, sent me a four-page letter as a birthday gift many years ago. Her letter is still savoured as a "tribute to me." She suggested that her "memory letter" was a lasting alternative to big ticket gift items. Once you have written your letter, mail it! Don't let time slip away stealing unspoken thoughts of love.

I have another friend whose challenge is to raise positive kids in a negative world. Each year she tucks her birthday card from me into her purse until her next birthday. Her daughter told me this, and I was astonished – another reminder of the power and the blessing of an encouraging word.

Go to a church library and find Gary Smalley and John Trent's *The Gift of the Blessing*. This book was a life-changer for me and many others. It has many practical tools to help you use the "word pictures" to get your message of encouragement across in a powerful way. Many people crave some small sign of approval, a word of recognition and an honest expression of appreciation for the good we see in them or their work.

Think about the priceless gift of encouragement as you draft your Christmas letter, or search for that perfect gift. Take time, thought and care in the words you share, and you may give the gift that lasts a lifetime.

THE GIFT OF A VISIT
DECEMBER 1996

Well Mom, what would you like for Christmas?" "Happy healthy children who are content with what they have!" But there is one other thing, how about a visit!

I dropped in yesterday for a cup of tea with my friend while my son was at hockey practice. I did not give advance notice, but I was welcomed with open arms. The encouragement and loving conversation shared over a spontaneous cup of tea will keep my emotional batteries well charged through this current cold snap!

Is it my imagination, or are we losing the art of visiting? My sense is that people feel they need a specific invitation to come to my home. We don't get many drop-in visitors other than those pesky salespeople, who actually are great to visit with if you give them a chance!

Perhaps people assume we are too busy, and don't have time for a visit. I'd like to dispel that myth with "don't assume anything!" Call ahead if you're not comfortable with just dropping in.

I'm ashamed that I usually see my neighbour just once a year, when we come in costumes for treats! My other neighbour is delighted to share tea, but usually just gets a wave as I trek by to run another errand in town. What is going to make us stop, to take time to build relationships?

Ask yourself if you can remember what colour of socks or sweatshirt you received last Christmas. I bet you're more likely to remember the laughter, caroling or chatter around the festive table. Some of you may have experienced no human connection at all, and long for a visit.

We all need to be affirmed, understood and appreciated. That can happen with a visit over the telephone, a letter, or being there "in the flesh." Phone calls and letters can keep the relationship flowing, but a personal visit is a special gift.

Visits let us see people in the context of their surroundings. We can pick up lots of clues as to how they are really doing, and what they need. A casual drop-in visit this summer to a woman who has a greenhouse, gave me a great place to share my bedding plant containers. Another spontaneous visit on a backyard deck was a time of "walking alongside" a couple struggling with the ups and downs of depression. We were unaware of their pain, until we stopped to visit.

Visits to see seniors can help their loneliness, but also teach your family lots in the process. I am eager to hear stories of "life in the old country" from my friend Susie, as she can teach me to appreciate my husband's heritage. As snow and cold capture people in their homes we can share the gift of friendship with our visits.

Christmas gatherings may be the "mega-visit" of the season, as we try to catch up with family and friends in one place. I'd encourage you to visit those you care about in the "off-season" as well.

Don't load yourself with the guilt of whom you "should" go and visit. I had intended to visit a friend in the hospital; unfortunately, she died an hour before I got there. Thankfully, I was comforted by the previous home visits, where I had enjoyed her fellowship.

Call a friend, mail that letter, and give the gift of a visit – soon!

THE GIFT OF LAUGHTER
DECEMBER 1997

"Love makes the world go round, but laughter keeps you from getting dizzy." – Victor Borge

The birthday card from my sister this year had a picture of two rosy-cheeked brown haired little girls linked arm in arm. The caption read "Remember when we were little, and it was the big people who had all the fun?" Inside the card reads "Are we having fun yet?" Amazingly, this was the exact question I put to my husband in the late throws of harvest.

My sister has a wonderful sense of humour, and finds fun everywhere. My goal is to find more balance in my life. I'm trying to lighten up, too. Laughter is the shock absorber that absorbs the blows of life.

At a provincial farm women's conference, Vancouver therapist Carol Ann Fried, presented "Laughing Matters, and Jest for the Health of It" – practical ideas on how to laugh it up and spread the merriment in your personal and professional life. Fried challenged me to create brief moments of fun throughout my day, and encourage others to have fun along with me. I invested in a $4–pair of Groucho Marx glasses with hairy eyebrows, nose and mustache...unsuspecting shoppers at my local grocery store would soon have a laugh!

A great belly laugh shared with family and friends is a wonderful blessing. Laughing draws in oxygen, increasing circulation and respiration. It boosts the immune system, and generates those "happy hormones" called endorphins that make us feel good.

Friends make a business of helping others have more fun and play in all of life's arenas. If you're short of cash for gifts this month, think of small creative ways to give the gift of laughter. A friend of mine who is recovering from depression shared a cassette called "Lighten Up" by Sandy Queen. Queen says, "take your job seriously, but take yourself lightly." When people ask "How are you?" respond with "Better and better!" It will drive them to ask "What drugs are you taking?"

Watching comedies together as a family, doing skits or charades, or playing silly games together can help the whole family lighten up. Wellness happens when we grow and develop through youthful traits like the giggles.

Having fun is a cheap, legal and happy way to live longer. Fried's five fulfilling fundamentals are:

- **Have as much fun as possible.** Fun = laughter. Pranks like hanging lingerie on the door hooks of the bank manager's office can create a laugh. Be positive, and use "non-toxic" jokes. Keep a funny book or log of the hilarious things your kids say.

- **Breathe more often.** Relax and practice "inverse paranoia" – believing that the world is out to do you good!

- **Perform random acts of kindness or senseless acts of beauty.** Being kind makes a big difference. When we feel good we tend to do good.

> *"A cheerful look brings joy to the heart, and good news gives health to the bones."* – Proverbs 15:30

- **Practice "funnel" vision.** Look outwards at the big picture and see all the good things around you. Recognize people around you.

- **Live this moment.** Start small by doing little things to be playful. Celebrate with those dear to you. And as Peter Hanson, author of *The Joy of Stress,* says "worry efficiently."

Laughter keeps us sane, healthier and helps us keep life in perspective. It can also take the hard edge off parental discipline. Take a play break with your family this Christmas. Go tobogganing and have a winter picnic together. Stick great jokes on the fridge. Pick names of secret family members to shower with random acts of kindness. Clean snow off a stranger's car. Play a kazoo to adjourn your next meeting. Dig into the dress-up box and don a new wig or wacky accessory!

Spread the gift of laughter, it's a gift your kids can't break! Create special family memories this Christmas. May light-heartedness, elation and joy be made real before your glistening eyes this year. May your family be blessed with love, joy and laughter this year.

The Gift of Simplicity
December 1998

> *"Glory to God in the highest, and on earth peace to men on whom his favor rests ... Mary treasured up all these things and pondered them in her heart."* Luke 2:14,19 (NIV)

As Christmas approaches you may be feeling like the business women in my stress workshop who have plotted to make their lives much simpler this year. The mere mention of "Christmas is coming" sends out panic waves!

In light of all the human tragedy and suffering after Hurricane Mitch in Central America, we have few problems to worry about! Search the pondering of your heart this year and ask yourself, "Am I too busy achieving and collecting stuff ... am I forgetting about connecting to what is really important?" In other words, are you overworking and under-relating?

Linus Mundy, author of *Keep-life-simple Therapy,* says "the gift of simplicity is appreciating the essence of life, freeing our resources and minds from anxiety over "stuff," caring about people, and enjoying our oneness with God." I heartily agree.

Popular books like *Don't Sweat the Small Stuff* and *Simple Abundance* encourage us to relax and slow down. We don't find simplicity because we clutter our lives with far more things and activities than we actually need.

I remember the day my *Martha Stewart Living* decorating magazine renewal coincided with a plea for the children in Sudan. Somehow the $40 sent to alleviate hunger was much more gratifying than money to generate more ways to collect things for my home. I canceled *Martha.*

You want simplicity in your life. Do you have to start living like the Amish in southern Ontario – No. "The spiritual discipline of simplicity is a compassionate and faithful response to world need, injustice and God's call to serve him above everyone and everything else. The source of simplicity is a deep inner reality of God's presence ... peace!"

Stephen Covey's bestseller *First Things First* urges us to put in the big rocks of our lives first – the important things such as relationships, and planning. People who seek simplicity and peace learn to choose between what is important, and what can wait; between what is of great value and what is of little consequence.

At Christmas, building family memories is of great value, and sharing the joy of knowing the peace of Christ's love in one's heart. Moments spent reflecting on the blessings or trials that helped you stretch this year help feed the hunger of our souls.

It's time to sit still around a fire or under the heavenly blanket of stars, to observe, reflect, to absorb, to enjoy, and to learn. "Ah ... if only" you quip to yourself. Why not?

Each of us needs a gentle reminder to take good care of our self, so that our wells are filled, and able to fill others. Asking family members what they truly expect of Christmas celebrations may help keep your well of excitement full for the season. Buying baking, or having the grandkids sift flour alongside you may be a start. Simplify the amount of decorating or gourmet extravaganzas planned. A letter of blessing from one heart to another is priceless compared to collecting more stuff that needs dusting.

I'm a great fan of nourishing books such as the Bible, *Simply Living in a Complex World* by David Irvine and *Plain and Simple – A Woman's Journey to the Amish* by Sue Bender.

Here are some simple gifts to give yourself and others this Christmas:

- Send love ... speak it, write it, celebrate it with affection. Love letters, cards or journals.

- Say "no"... set boundaries on your time and expectations. Don't get steamed about having everything "perfect" or "homemade."

- Value spiritual things over material things. Where is your real treasure?

- Know when you have enough, reduce the "stuff" and clutter in your life. Read Don Aslett's *Clutter's Last Stand.*

- Be nurtured by nature and your creator. Smell the pines, breath deeply the crisp air, and hear the snow crunch!

- Live in the present moment, even as you recognize past losses, and hope for the future.

- Be real. "To thine own self be true"... a very freeing truth for a meaningful life.

- Feed your soul with solitude, listen to God's prompting.

- Cultivate an attitude of gratitude, practice being content.

- Balance what you are achieving in your work with connecting in meaningful relationships.
- Rediscover the joy of quiet conversation, laughter in stories and games.
- Light those candles you've been storing.

As you celebrate the joy of the birth of Jesus each day of the year, I wish you peace and happiness sharing the gift of simplicity. God loves you. Relax, reflect, and be good to yourself.

PONDER AND PLANT:

How have you simplified your life? _____

_____

_____

_____

_____

_____

_____

_____

_____

_____

_____

_____

_____

_____

THE GIFT OF YOUR PRESENCE
DECEMBER 1999

"The Lord replied, My Presence will go with you, and I will give you rest." – Exodus 33:14 (NIV).

The thing I love about winter blizzards is that the demands of the outside world shut down, and you are trapped (hopefully at home) with your family and no schedule.

Snowstorms give us "time margin" a term coined by Dr. Richard Swenson, author of *Margin – Restoring Emotional, Physical, Financial, and Time Reserves to Overloaded Lives.*

For more than seven years I have been encouraging farm families to balance their lives in a complex world. We may be so overloaded with activities that there are few blank spaces on our kitchen calendar or in our day-timers. No time for family, or even ourselves. "Many people have not heard from themselves for a long, long time," says Robert Banks.

Sit down and ask yourself: "Am I interruptible? Do I have time for unscheduled things in my life?"

If my heart's desire is to be loving and useful I need to give family and friends the gift of my presence. "Usefulness is nine-tenths availability," says Swenson.

Besides waiting for a blizzard, how can I be available?

1. Cancel things that aren't the "main things". Funerals are a good reminder that many things can be cancelled in order to spend time with people. Saying, "No, not at this time" gives you permission to focus on the priorities in your life.

2. Mark off some time margin in your plan for the week. Keep some days blank. These days of grace can be offered to God, family, and friends. I have a friend who keeps Wednesdays open for visiting others.

3. Delight in what Swenson calls "divine interruption." This summer our long-lost caravan cousins from Denver descend-

ed on us wanting to connect our family histories. We now keep track of their adventures across North America by e-mail. Canceling our weekend plans to reconnect with lost family was a wonderful blessing to us all.

Giving the gift of your presence to a friend and a good cause won't hurt ... you'll be achieving some wonderful things, and creating relationships at the same time.

Our church Easter banner was stitched with great care and conversation in a two-day project with my quilting friend. In May, a two-day band trip to Regina with our daughter was a special time to focus on fun with her. A day spent judging jellies in June was time to reconnect with a home economist chum.

Connecting with my creative side, I spent three August days sitting in ditches, and near sloughs painting at Art Camp with a close artist friend. I gave my local M.L.A. my support by attending his election poll in September. In October, I learned a new baking skill, making Mennonite double buns called "Zwiebach" with my "adopted mother."

Making another person's life rich is spelled T-I-M-E. If you gave me the choice between a present that requires dusting, and the option to spend a day with you having creative fun. I'd pick you!

Paper coupon promises for walks around the snowy shelter-belt, pie and tea at your house, exploring the ravines together, or cropping photos for a scrapbook, are wonderful gift ideas. A letter of encouragement written on special paper with an invitation to spend time together is priceless. Watching your children or grandchildren play hockey is a wonderful gift of your presence.

Could you give yourself to family or friends, uninterrupted for a whole day? I agree with Swenson that everyone needs God time, personal time, family time and sharing with friends time.

As you reflect on God's goodness in sending you His son, be still with God's love. Give God time. Create some white space "blizzards" of time margin on your calendars. Your family will never be the same again when you give them the gift of your presence. Bing Crosby may have been "dreaming of a white Christmas" but I'm excited about a "white calendar!"

THE GIFT OF PEACE
DECEMBER 2001

I always shake my head and laugh when the Christmas Wish Book appears in the middle of September! Like many moms, I hide the catalogue, hoping to avoid relentless discussions about "all I want for Christmas is…"

Christmas is the celebration of the birth of Jesus Christ, the Prince of Peace. This year as families join to celebrate and read "Glory to God in the highest, and on earth peace, good will toward men" (Luke 1:14), we have some new reflections. Our world is not at peace. Many families are unsettled and fear their future. Being a grain farmer in the middle of the bald prairie seems like a blessing when compared to fighting for daily survival in the inner-city or a third-world country.

Canada is a rich nation, but our country is full of "poor" people who think they need to own more stuff! Plato said "Poverty consists not in the decrease of one's possession but in the increase of one's greed." We are caught up in the peace-busting expectation that we need more toys, turf, trucks and trinkets. Our expectations are stirring up discontent in our families. The unsettling truth is that more is never enough, and our malcontent destroys any possibility of personal peace.

"Life's goodies are truly good when God provides them in His way and in His time. They are enslaving when we demand them," writes Ron Hutchcraft in *Surviving the Storms of Stress*. Here are three areas where you may be letting your expectations wipe out your peace:

- **Possession expectations.** How long is your Christmas list? "Godliness with contentment is great gain. For we brought nothing into the world and we can take nothing out of it. But if we have food and clothing, we will be content with that," says 1 Timothy 6: 6-8 (NIV).

- **People expectations.** Are you living in a state of chronic frustration because your family and friends just don't measure up? How sad it is, there are fragmented families this Christmas who can't speak to each other. They don't want to be satisfied with accepting others just the way they are, unconditionally loving them. We all have imperfections! Why do you keep expecting perfection from your son or daughter-in-law?

- **Performance expectations:** "Performance drives us to stressful schedules, sacrifices and compromises when our worth becomes identified with our work," says Hutchcraft. I agree. We are human beings, not human doings. Our value lies in our character and ability to love, not in how much we achieve or perform. If you are a workaholic farmer, you have been avoiding building relationships for too long. Peace will not come through more chores, it comes with commitment to building healthy relationships with God, and the people you love.

"Seek peace and pursue it," says Psalm 34:14. Peaceful living resists self-induced stress, but grows from the things stretch us. Suffering with ill-health and becoming well again teaches us compassion and understanding to encourage others. Hard financial times help us focus our true priorities and rejoice when the harvest is better. When a "peace-pursuer" understands he is in training rather than in trouble, he can relax, even under fire! As the Bible says, we can "endure hardship as discipline … no discipline seems pleasant at the time, but painful. Later on however, it produces a harvest of righteousness and peace for those who have been trained by it" (Hebrews12:7, 11).

This Christmas you may be feeling snowed under by an avalanche of stress. Peace seems foreign. God brings peace to our hearts through the gift of His Son, Jesus, the Prince of Peace. May you unwrap the best gift this Christmas, "for He Himself is our peace" (Ephesians 2:14).

THE GIFT OF SILENCE
DECEMBER 2000

"Everyone should be quick to listen, slow to speak and slow to become angry." – James 1:19 (NIV)

T hanks for the way you always listen...not just with an open mind...but with such a caring heart," said the card. My theme for 2000 has been to try new ways of enjoying the quiet, listening to my own thoughts, holding my tongue longer, and seeking the Spirit's prompting.

Do you automatically start your day with the noise of the radio while contemplating how long you can stay in bed before chores, or the school bus's arrival? Do you need to have noise while you eat your cereal, milk the cows, or run an errand? Cell phones, radios, TV, CD's in our computers are filling our ears incessantly. Why do we fear silence?

I worked hard this year to try to be a better listener, and more creative. *The Artist's Way*, by Julia Cameron, encouraged me to deprive myself of all media input for an entire week. I survived. I actually enjoyed being quiet in the combine for 13 hours straight watching the hawks vie for the field mice, and the coyote come for a visit. "Many people haven't heard from themselves for a long time," quipped a time management writer. I've come to appreciate quiet surroundings, listening to my thoughts, taking note of who and what comes to mind. Silence can be a creative companion.

It all started with moving a $25-well-padded chair to a corner of our kitchen. Weekday mornings, and in the wonderful low light of pre-supper simmering I hit the chair for some journaling, Bible reading and prayer. I am attempting to fill my mind with a rich attachment to God where He gives guidance, perspective and balance. Richard Foster's *Celebration of Discipline* encourages us to recreate silences to counteract the noise, hurry and crowds of contemporary society.

"This you can try at home. Find a secret place where you can be idle. A place where you can breath naturally and untether yourself from the world, from all threads of concern. Where you can slip into silence. Think of this as a descent into stillness. Just be there, no place else. Here patience is crucial. Because when you make up your mind to stay put and enter silence you'll begin to confront a raucous interior with inane inner conversation, absurd vignettes, weird little movies, most of them "talkies." All this will conspire to make you take some form of refuge. But resist, because this is when God begins to speak.

In the end silence is for prayer, for secret prayer to the Father; and this secret prayer is listening. The discipline of silence is not so we can escape from a noisy world. Instead it allows us to live in a noisy world. Silence is not absence, it is a presence; it is a companion," says Steve Berg of Edmonton's Hope Mission.

Give the gift of being an attentive, listening companion. Elaine St. James, author of *Simplify Your Life* concludes: "Stop trying to change people. People change when they are good and ready. What people really want is a supportive ear. Now, I just listen. Boy, has that simplified my life! And it has freed up a lot of energy to spend in more enjoyable and productive pursuits."

How we listen to others depends a great deal on how we were listened to as a child says Tom Brown, a counselor from England. Brown conducts 10-hour listening workshops. I learned from Tom that a good phrase to capture the essence of what your friend tells you is: "What do you think is most important in what you have been saying? Is there any action you want to take? What are you feeling at this moment about what you have just shared?"

When I choose to be silent, and really listen with a noble, generous heart, I am like a rich, dark seedbed, ready to witness growth. I can "hug with my eyes" as the speaker pores out her story, giving the gift of full attention. As I listen without judging or interrupting, the storyteller gains insight, understanding and growth.

Listening to the silence can help you get to know yourself, and God's still small voice. When you turn off the noise you'll be able to remember those who come to mind "out of the blue." There is likely a weary parent who would be deeply blessed with some quiet solitude, or sharing their story with you. Seniors who have a large bank of quiet in their day delight in reminiscing. Listen to their vivid oral history. Your spouse likely needs a good shoulder rub, toes tickled, and your full eye contact ... with the TV remote hidden!

And how about yourself? Have you been listening to the inner being of your soul? Is silence a companion that makes you feel nurtured? What are you pushing out of your mind by continually cramming your head with noise and hurry?

We show great love when we listen. Christmas time celebrates the birth of a child, Jesus, the Son of God. Jesus was happy to listen. He didn't judge anyone unworthy of His presence. If your world seems too chaotic, choose silence as a companion, and give the gift of listening to God, yourself, family and friends.

THE GIFT OF NEXT YEAR
DECEMBER 2002

"Be strong and take heart, all you who hope in the Lord."
– Psalm 31:24 (NIV)

"I hope all is well with you and your family. It is the most miserable year for farming. I drove through the countryside and saw every kind of crop still standing or lying in swathes. Now snow covers the ground. I call it the year that didn't happen — we had no spring, no summer and no fall, as we know it. But my life is good and blessed."

As my friend from Saskatchewan Landing wrote, it has been a tough year for many farm families. Finding my "gift theme" for this column has been a struggle, because farm families in different areas have had different outcomes.

According to Gary Smalley's *Better or Best* book, we need to create a toolbox of living, for helping us reflect on our life, relationships and coping skills. We need:

- **Courage** – That inner commitment to pursue a worthwhile goal without giving up hope. Farmers have always been tagged as "next year" people. We hope that the prices, weather and crops will be better next year.

- **Persistence** – We continue to pursue a goal until it is achieved. When I read accounts of how Albertan families had fought off three consecutive tough years, I was impressed with their persistence to find new income with trucking jobs, cut costs, and focus on stronger family relationships. As Romans 5:3-5 (NIV) tells us: "We know that suffering produces perseverance; perseverance, character; and character, hope. And hope does not disappoint us, because God has poured out his love into our hearts by the Holy Spirit, whom he has given us."

- **Gratefulness** – My Saskatchewan friend expressed her thankfulness for feeling blessed. Maybe it is time to reflect upon all of our blessings of the past year and be grateful for the family who loves and cares for us, and fills our emotional bank account even when the financial account is in the red.

- **Calmness** – A stormy time can drive us to panic, or to our knees. Do you have the inner peace that allows you to respond quietly to a stressful situation without fear? Our daughter is overseas and will not be home for Christmas. My prayers for her protection and happiness are being answered. My peace doesn't come from worldly things; it comes from the very heart of God.

- **Gentleness** – Show tender consideration for the feelings of others. This may be the most precious gift you can give this Christmas. We don't like to fail or disappoint our families. Good farm managers are crushed under the weight of debt and limited incomes, yet they are highly esteemed by God no matter what happens.

- **Unselfish love** – This is the genuine loving act of meeting other's needs prior to your own personal needs. Many parents portray unselfish love everyday as they work long hours to provide the basics for their families.

Our feelings tend to follow our thinking and our actions. "IF ONLY" … are two small but powerful words that can keep you down. Here are some prompting questions to focus on the gift of a good next year.

1) What did I accomplish in the last year?

2) What were my biggest disappointments in the last year?

3) What did 2002 teach me? State what you learned as advice to yourself.

4) What three things did I learn that would make the most difference by putting them into action in 2003?

5) What limitations or assumptions about myself lead me to failure rather than to success? My frustrations in life are these … and this is the way I want to change the way I look at myself next year.

6) What are the most important cherished beliefs or values I have? List these on a card and keep them close to your calendar or day timer (e.g., compassion, intimacy, contribution, achieving, play, making money, creativity, taking care of myself, etc.).

7) What focus do I want to put on my roles as spouse, parent, worker, friend, and community person?

8) What are my goals for each role? How can I achieve them?

The gift of next year is to look ahead with hope. You balance living today according to your cherished beliefs – working, loving, and living with a positive outlook for the future you purposely desire and plan. "For I know the plans I have for you declares the Lord, plans to prosper you and not to harm you, plans to give you hope and a future. Then you will call upon me and come and pray to me, and I will listen to you. You will seek me and find me when you seek me with all your heart" (Jeremiah 29:11-13 NIV).

> *"Give, and it will be given to you. A good measure, pressed down, shaken together and running over, will be poured into your lap. For with the measure you use, it will be measured to you."* – Luke 6:38 (NIV)

THE GIFT OF CONTENTMENT
DECEMBER 2003

"We can be content because God will never leave us no matter how tough the situation is." – Hebrews 13:5-6 (Msg)

The *Sears Christmas Wish Book* arrived in September, but the kids didn't think of asking for it until Thanksgiving weekend! The season for celebrating the birth of Jesus draws families and friends together. It also creates a lot of tension and worry when folks are overwhelmed with trying to fulfill the wants and wishes of others. As I pondered the title of this year's "gift" column, the word that kept hitting home was contentment.

My eighty-something mother-in-law came to this country as a young toddler with parents, siblings and a suitcase. She now reviews her life story with a thankful heart, content to share what she has with others in need: her health, her wealth, her wisdom and her cookies! "When you have enough, the basics, it is good to be content," is the gist of what she believes.

I asked a few other farmers this season about what they would say about contentment. One fellow had tears well up as he awaits the surgeon's report. Others just shrugged their shoulders and said, "It's been a tough year ... 50 years of work are now in jeopardy."

Circumstances may be critical, yet God is still in control. Is this a key to being content no matter what life crisis tries to crush you? This season marks a celebration of the birth of a saviour. Jesus came to give us the gift of salvation and the hope of eternal life. Being content during this season calls us to reflect and cherish the spiritual gift we can choose to open. We each have the chance to accept and open up a vital dynamic relationship with God for our lives, for the present, and for our eternal well being.

In the Bible, Paul writes to the Philippians about contentment: "I have learned to be content whatever the circumstances. I know what it is to be in need, and I know what it is to have plenty. I have learned the secret of being content in any and every situation, whether well fed or hungry, whether living in plenty or in want. I can do everything through him who gives me strength" (Philippians 4:11-13 NIV). Wow...what a gift!

There might not be a new Christmas dress this year, or a holiday trip, or the hockey equipment. The gifts under the tree might be letters of love, thankfulness and affirmation. It might be a cup of tea with a neighbour shared in the spirit of friendship and caring.

Contentment to celebrate in a different way may move Dad to build a snow pile for the kids or a backyard ice rink. Mom might dig to the back of the attic or closet for long-forgotten treasures that need new light and perspective. Some gifts may be a family heirloom or book that needs to be passed along to the next generation. The kids might want to challenge Grandpa to a game of cards or monopoly.

"Relationships, not achievement or the acquisition of things, are what matter most in life," says Rick Warren, author of the Christian book *Purpose Driven Life.* I agree. If we trust in God, we can be content with what we have and not worry.

Bake cookies and decorate them together. Go skating, sledding, trail riding, skiing or walking. Look up! Share moments round a scrapbook, photo album or family history book. Tell stories. Build a bonfire and roast wieners. Laugh lots.

You have many tools and resources in your home to be content. Keep the *Wish Book* on the shelf this year. Open the good book and be content in going God's way.

THE GIFT OF INTERRUPTION
December 2004

My cell phone rings a musical dance tone as I wrap up a call on my office line. My son needs his Physics binder delivered to his locker within 30 minutes. I have two choices: to get really frosted and say "No, you need to get yourself better organized" or I can say, "I'll be there."

I ignored the responsible parenting books...as I was "forced" to go to town. I did my errands and checked the white card at the post office that notifies us of people who have passed away. One woman quipped she was "glad to be walking in the cool weather just to find out she was still alive, and not posted on the card at the post office!"

Funerals are life's ultimate interruptions. Death does not call ahead to see if your calendar is full. Think back of the celebrations of life that you've witnessed this past year. I felt blessed to attend the funerals of a elderly dad and mom who died within months of each other. It was a gift to hear their children reflect their legacy of love, and a gracious reminder to parent our children well with prayer.

Interruptions are a part of life, but rarely do we see them as a gift. I was interrupted last December on the curb at the Toronto airport when a well-dressed woman in a black cape approached me about a shuttle. We were both headed to the same hotel, and she graciously offered me shelter by sharing her room. She blessed me with her generosity, and is now a wonderful mentor and friend.

Today a woman at the post office asked if I was busy. I said "I was being intentional, not busy." Busy people whirl and get mad when they have to take into account someone else's agenda. Intentional people keep their eyes on the prize, but know that detours can be a blessing.

Air Canada's glycol shortage interrupted my life during a blizzard in April 2003. The de-icing fluid was gone, so they closed the airport. Again, I met someone needing help. He spoke only French and, in my broken French, I negotiated a better plane ticket for his family to Calgary. He was so grateful that later he sent me the shirt off his back.

At the baggage claim we connected again, and minutes later when we realized we were stranded, his family shared a taxi with me. The flight interruption had given me a tangible way to be a "gift" to a stranger.

For those affected by the "Mad Cow" crisis, I can't imagine what the interruption of cross-border cattle traffic has done to your cash flow. I take heart in the stories of creative marketers who have found another way to sell beef. It may be really tough at your home this Christmas. Can you see an opportunity in this crucial interruption in your way of life? Have you considered an exit strategy? Do you think this interruption has a purpose in getting your attention to focus on what really matters to you and your family?

It is not polite to interrupt other people when they are talking. However, if you have some tough issues that need to be exposed, it might be time to interrupt the talkative ones in the family, and get some airtime. Farm families who I've coached this year have found those passionate conversations to be life-changing. They aren't easy. I encourage you to check yourself as you celebrate and converse with family and friends. Is everyone able to share and feel cared for?

Would you be willing to interrupt your comfortable lifestyle and help others? Examples of meaningful interruptions are everywhere. A reader called looking for ideas on how to have more meaning in his life. He's met his farming goals and is looking for new challenges. We have friends who farm in the summer and help repair homes in hurricane country down south. This year, they've found a housing project in Hawaii to serve others and enjoy the sunshine! Another couple left this farming community for training and are now helping Romania's poorest people.

Seeing the commitment and sacrifice of a couple dedicated to serving the poor challenges us to live more sacrificially and interrupts our buying patterns.

What would it mean to your family if you interrupted gift buying this year and bought nothing? What ways could you celebrate by parking your credit cards in favour of other activities?

I love interruptions that are met with delight. It is fun to drop in on friends to reconnect and share your love. Impromptu lunch dates can set creative juices flowing for new projects. Lousy weather can force us to change our work plans and consider times of rejuvenation.

I hope that the interruptions in your life call you to a place where, as Frederick Buechner says, "your deep joy meets the world's deep hunger."

BIBLIOGRAPHY

Bridges, William. Managing Transitions: *Making the Most of Change.* NewYork: Perseus, 1991.

Canfield, Jack and Mark Victor Hansen. *The Aladdin Factor.* Berkeley Books, l995.

Callaway, Phil. *Making Life Rich Without Any Money.* Harvest House, l998.

Callaway, Phil. *Who Put My Life on Fast Forward?* Harvest House, 2002.

Cameron, Julia. *The Artist's Way.* Tarcher/Putnam, l992.

Carlson, Dr.Richard. *Don't Sweat the Small Stuff.* New York: Hyperion, 1997.

Carter, Jimmy. *The Virtues of Aging.* New York: Balantine, l998.

Chapman, Gary. *The Five Love Languages.* Northfield Publishing, 1995.

Crary, Elizabeth. *Pick Up Your Socks and Other Skills Growing Children Need.* Parenting Press. 1990.

DeGaetano, Gloria. *Television and the Lives of Our Children.* Train of Thought Publishing, l994.

Dembe, Dr. Sharon. *Passionate Longevity.* Toronto: Macmillan Canada, 1995.

Edwards, Betty. *Drawing on the Right Side of the Brain.* Jeremy P.Tarcher, l979.

Farmer, Dr.Val. *Honey, I Shrunk the Farm, A Rural Stress Survival Guide.* Gwinner ND: McCleery and Sons Publishing, 2000.

Gelatt, H.B. & Carol Gelatt. *Creative Decision Making Using Positive Uncertainty.* MenloPark: Crisp Press, l999.

Graham, Karen. *Meals for Good Health.* Portage: Paper Birch Publishing, l998.

Gray, John. *Men are from Mars Women are from Venus.* Harper Collins, 1992.

Harley,William. *His Needs Her Needs.* Revell, 1986.

Harris, Joshua. *I Kissed Dating Goodbye.* Oregon: Multnomah, 1997.

Irvine, David. *Simple Living in a Complex World … Balancing Life's Achievements.* Calgary: RedstoneVentures, l997 (now published by Wiley).

Jeffers, Susan. *Feel the Fear and Do it Anyway.* New York: Ballantine, 1987.

Krebs Hirsch, Sandra. *Soultypes.* New York: Hyperion, 1998.

LaHaye, Tim and Bob Phillips. *Anger is a Choice.* Grand Rapids, MI: Zondervan, 2002.

Leman, Dr. Kevin. *Bringing Up Kids Without Tearing Them Down.* Delacorte Press, l993.

Ortberg, John. *If You Want to Walk on Water You've Got to Get Out of The Boat.* Zondervan, 2001

Pipher, Mary. R*eviving Ophelia; Saving the Selves of Adolescent Girls.* Ballantine Books, l994

McColm, Michelle. *Adoption Reunions.* Second Story Press, 1993.

Mcullough, Bonnie Runyan and Susan Walker Monson. *401 Ways to Get Kids to Work at Home.* St. Martin Press, l981

Mason, Mike. *Champagne for the Soul.* Waterbrook Press, 2003.

Maurer, Rick. *Why Don't You Want What I Want?* Austin Atlanta: Bard Press, 2002.

Robinson, Bryan E. *Chained to the Desk-A Guidebook for Workaholics.* New York: NY University Press, l998.

Richardson, Cheryl. *Life Makeovers.* New York: Broadway Books, 2000.

Scott, Susan. *Fierce Conversations ... Achieving Success at Work and in Life One Conversation at a Time.* New York: Viking, 2002.

Smalley, Gary, and John Trent. *The Blessing Workbook.* Nashville: Thomas Nelson, 1993.

Stern, Ellen Sue. R*unning on Empty Meditations for Indispensable Women.* Bantam, l992.

Swenson, Dr. Richard. *Margin.* Colorado Springs, Colorado, Navpress, 1992.

Tannen, Deborah. *You Just Don't Understand.* New York: Ballantine, 1990.

Waterhouse, Debra. *Outsmarting the Mid-life Fat Cell ...Winning Weight Control Strategies for Women Over 35 to Stay Fit Through Menopause.* Time Warner, l994.

Weiner-Davis, Michelle. *Divorce Busting.* New York: Summit Books, 1992.

Wilson Shaef, Anne. *Meditations for Women Who Do Too Much.* San Francisco: Harper Collins, 1990.

CONTACT THE AUTHOR

KEYNOTES AND SEMINARS

Elaine Froese is a high-energy writer and certified coach who speaks from the heart. She delivers entertaining common sense content as keynote speeches and seminars to various groups who want to change their lives, or business. She helps clients get "unstuck" by looking at the business, family or communication issues that weigh them down. Her professional coaching training from the Hudson Institute of Santa Barbara gives her the tools to help families in business move forward for transition and succession. She also finds her certificate in conflict resolution helpful for "discussing the undiscussbull."™

Elaine's strengths are communication, empathy, optimism, life-long learning, and the ability to win others over. She uses these skills as a mediator, facilitator, master of ceremonies, coach and keynote speaker.

- As a farmer, she understands the agri-business culture.
- As a parent, she appreciates the gift of family.
- As a professional speaker and writer, she provides a forum for intentional change and success in transition.

Readers are energizing ... write us!

Writers appreciate knowing how their stories have impacted others. Elaine is delighted to know how her writing has helped people be intentional about planting hope and making positive changes in their lives. Please send your stories and comments to elaine@elainefroese.com.

To order more copies call 1-866-848-8311

To order more copies of this book, go to www.elainefroese.com or inquire about large orders at elaine@elainefroese.com.

TESTIMONIALS

"Elaine's sincerity and commitment to helping farm families has no limits. She works hard at connecting with her audience – whether it is a one-on-one coaching situation, speaking to a group of hundreds, or writing a column with a readership of thousands. She is one of the few people I know who 'walks what she talks'."
– Donna Hastings, CEO and President of the
Canadian Association of Farm Advisors

*"I loved your book Elaine!
It's easy to read, just like Reader's Digest."*
– Betty Turner, Farm Woman

"Elaine Froese is a respected catalyst for Canadian agriculture. Her personal experience as a farmer and mother combined with her great story-telling abilities make her a sought after speaker and an ambassador for stronger farms and stronger farm families."
– Kim McConnell, CEO of AdFarm

*"Elaine has the spiritual gift of encouragement.
She is able to touch our hearts by using this gift."*
– John Smith, farmer and CEO of Seed Depot

"Elaine's passion for the challenges of life on the Prairies makes this a particularly powerful message. She combines a keen understanding of the issues with practical tools for managing the forces of change. This is a 'must read' for anyone grappling with tough choices and important decisions about the future on the farm, on the prairie, or in one's life."
– Dr. Pam McLean, CEO, The Hudson Insitute